LIFE IS NOT WORK
WORK IS NOT LIFE

Simple Reminders for Finding
Balance in a 24–7 World

ROBERT K. JOHNSTON
AND
J. WALKER SMITH

WILDCAT CANYON PRESS
A Division of Circulus Publishing Group, Inc.
Berkeley, California

Life Is Not Work; Work Is Not Life: Simple Reminders for Finding Balance in a 24–7 World

Copyright © 2001 by Robert K. Johnston and J. Walker Smith

Photo of JWS by Smith's Studio of Photography, Stone Mountain, GA.
Photo of RKJ by Don Milici.

Publisher: Tamara Traeder
Editorial Director: Roy M. Carlisle
Marketing Director: Carol Brown
Managing Editor: Leyza Yardley
Production Coordinator: Larissa Berry

Copyeditor: Jean Blomquist
Cover Design: Mary Beth Salmon
Interior Design and Typesetting:
   Margaret Copeland/Terragraphics

Typographic Specifications: Text in Arrus; headers in Trajan
Printed in the United States of America

Library of Congress Cataloging-in-Publication Data
Johnston, Robert K., 1945–
     Life is not work, work is not life : simple reminders for finding balance in a 24/7 world / by Robert K. Johnston & J. Walker Smith.
       p. cm.
     Includes bibliographical references.
     ISBN 1-885171-54-4 (alk. paper)
     1. Conduct of life—Quotations, maxims, etc. 2. Work—Quotations, maxims, etc. 3. Life—Quotations, maxims, etc. I. Smith, J. Walker. II. Title.

BJ1581.2.J645 2001
248.4—dc21
                                                                    00-069322

Distributed to the trade by Publishers Group West
10 9 8 7 6 5 4 3 2   05 04 03 02 01

*To my father, Roy Johnston, who continues at eighty-seven (!)
not only to have a successful career as a consulting engineer,
but an even more successful and balanced life.
He has modeled for me a life of work and play, worship
and service, family and friendships. Thanks.*
—Robert K. Johnston

*To Joy first and foremost, who has been steadfast by my
side throughout the years and who has enriched my life beyond
compare. And to the boatmen of the Grand Canyon Dories,
especially Roger, Shawn, Carol, and, most of all, Bronco,
whose work on the river makes it possible for me
to share in the enjoyment of life's most magnificent
natural treasure, and a place that is very special to me.*
—J. Walker Smith

CONTENTS

A WORD FROM ROB

"Living a life of extremes tends to produce good press but poor people." My dad probably didn't use these exact words, but this is the gist of what he counseled me when I was a teenager. I can remember wanting to stay out late into the night on my dates. My parents did not challenge me; they simply counseled me that balance was important in all of life, including my social life. And did I think that driving home at two in the morning showed moderation or balance? At that age, and with those hormones, I was not convinced I needed balance! But I also didn't have an answer for such common sense wisdom. Life *was* simply better when it had a rhythm and nonchalance. It didn't work to go on little to no sleep the next day. I couldn't play football as well or do as well in my studies. I was often out of sorts. Here is the germ idea that has developed into this book.

In graduate school, I picked a topic for my doctoral dissertation that would not only allow me to reflect on how the Christian faith might help us all understand the shape of human life, I selected a subject for my thesis that would allow me some personal balance as well. I wrote on the theological relevance of play! Most folk who are seriously religious know how to work hard; but do we know also how to play? Similarly, most graduate students work long hours, but many have little life beyond the library. I wanted something different. My topic allowed me to read countless novels as I got a suntan out on the lawn of the dormitory where I was a house-counselor. It encouraged me to take three months off one summer to go on an archeological dig in Israel. It propelled me to consider why people of faith should not only work, but play. And ironically, the playtime actually improved my work.

In the 1970's when I got my Ph.D., all the societal indicators suggested that the length of the average work week would continue to drop as it had for the last hundred years. It was assumed that our increasing leisure time would become a problem for many Americans. Thus, I believed that my writing would be relevant to those large groups of people who were being forced to retire early, or those who would be working four day weeks, or those who would have extra discretionary time given the labor-saving devices that were proliferating. But I was wrong.

By the eighties, things had changed. The futurists were singing a different song. The average work week had again begun to climb. This has continued over the last two decades, so that now we work on average over forty-seven hours a week. Moreover, we are working harder than ever even when we are not on the job, trying to squeeze a maximum number of fun things into our ever-tightening schedules. And labor saving devices haven't really produced more free time! Something, of course, has to give. For many this has been time with our children or our friends. For others it has been our sleep. We sense that our lives lack a proper rhythm or balance, but we seem caught in our expectations and obligations.

I have struggled like the rest of you. There are simply too many books and new ideas in the disciplines I teach to stay ahead of the curve, let alone be creative. If I am going to take my students with the seriousness they desire, I have few hours to write or research.

To help counter my workaholism, I have returned time and again to the advice of Ecclesiastes, the Old Testament sage: "Go, eat your bread with enjoyment, and drink your wine with a merry heart; for God has long approved what you do." (Ecclesiastes 9:7 *NRSV*) I fell in love with this short book as a teenager, and it remains my favorite biblical text. My first published paper was entitled "Confessions of a Workaholic." It was an appraisal of the wisdom of this writer, who argues that we can not find meaning on our own by working at mastering life, but must instead receive life from God as the fragile gift that it is.

My attempts to find balance in life have taken the form of protecting my larger life from work's incursions. Thus, our family has always taken a long vacation. I also have rejected the temptation to make those times away a "working" vacation. When my children were younger, I made it a policy not to do work at home until they were in bed. And I continue to set limits, some of which must seem quite arbitrary to others. I refuse, for example, to answer my e-mail every day, though I usually look at it. I don't have cable TV, because I already see too many movies at the theater and on video (I teach courses in theology and the movies). I don't even have a cell phone.

Such choices have nothing to do with the rightness or wrongness of e-mail, cable TV, or cell phones. Rather they have everything to do with trying to maintain a balance in my life, a balance between work and play, activity and rest, family and profession.

Some are arguing today that we are addicted to work. And it is a temptation. That addiction goes well beyond our job at work and our computers at home to include our commitment to incessant busy-ness in all of our lives. Even our play is not immune from this "bug." For all of us at times, it is as if we have no right to *be* if we are not constantly *doing* something, *producing* something, *making* something. Yet as we begin this new millennium, most of us have the common sense to know that such extremes produce skewed human beings. Despite our actions to the contrary, life is not work . . . and work is not life.

Like my father's advice to me as a teenager, this book is not meant to judge our overcommitments, but to remind us there is a better way. A healthy life has balance. We know this to be true, and yet we need the reminder. At least I do.

—*Robert K. Johnston*

A WORD FROM WALKER

I began my career in the seventies. I thought of work as a calling. I wanted to work hard, make a difference, and find fulfillment in what I achieved. I expected to realize most of what I wanted out of life through work, so it was not a big step for me to cross over into the workaholism that was de rigueur in the eighties and early nineties.

As my career in marketing research and consulting took off, I gave over more and more of my life to my work until my way of life became the epitome of the worst excesses of a work-saturated lifestyle. At my most excessive I was working eighty-plus hours a week while flying around the country on a seemingly endless succession of day trips that started at 5 A.M. and ended at midnight. The press for time and the stress that came with it were relentless. Sleep wasn't a luxury, it was a nuisance because it got in the way of work. The only meaningful brush I had with life outside of work occurred in airports. I used to joke that if it wasn't sold in an airport I couldn't buy it, and I bought more than my fair share of birthday gifts and anniversary presents at some store in a terminal on my way out the door to a meeting.

Work at this over the top level of intensity was its own reward for me. Nothing else in life seemed to compare to the stakes, the pace, the access, the impact, and the recognition of work. The allure of work held me spellbound and spurred me on to ever more immoderate extremes.

Today, my view of work is quite different. I am no less committed to work but now I have a commitment to life as well. In particular, I enforce strict limits on the sacrifices I will make for work. No longer will I allow work to seduce me into a reckless disregard of my health, my family, or my soul. I still see work as a calling, but having lived for so long with a life full of nothing but work, I know from personal experience that without a life to come home to, success at work is an empty achievement.

What broke the spell that work had over me was no one thing, no ecstatic moment of revelation and insight, no major crisis or sudden epiphany, no great escape. Rather, work lost its hold on me over time, through an accumulation of experiences, reflections, and regrets, until at long last I began the slow but steady process of reconstructing my way of life to fully accommodate a balance between life and work. I am still at it every single day.

I believe that my struggle with life and work is the same kind of struggle faced by most of us. Few of us change our outlooks or our lifestyles in one fell swoop. Such dramatic moments are not the stuff of our lives. For most of us, finding a way to balance work and life starts with a gradual erosion of our commitment to one way of life followed by an equally incremental reconstruction of a new way of life. This book is written for this kind of struggle.

There are few, if any, simple solutions to the problem of finding balance, and this book offers no pat recipes for success. Instead, this book shares personal stories and thoughts about the cares and the joys of life and work, which I hope will offer you some fresh ways to look at how you go about life and work. This book is intended as well to offer some reassurance that balance is a real possibility not a fantastic pipe dream. I've lived to tell about it, if you will, and this book relates many of the experiences and reflections that helped me rethink my own way of life.

Much of my struggle for balance has taken place in the shadow of my diabetes, a chronic disease that I've had since college. In my first job after graduate school I was asked to present an important study to the board of directors. During the discussion following my presentation I had a severe insulin reaction and passed out. When I finally came to and all was well again, I noticed that several of the directors looked pale and drawn. I had scared the wits out of them and this realization caused me to worry not about my health but that I had compromised my business standing with them. I resolved then and there to never allow anything like that to happen again even if it meant significantly relaxing how tightly and thus how well I controlled my diabetes.

For many years following that board of directors meeting, I deliberately kept my blood sugar high so that during meetings or while traveling I would never be at risk of having an insulin reaction because of low blood sugar. On average, my blood sugar level ran two to three times higher than normal, something I knew to be directly correlated with long-term complications. To steer clear of the scolding I always got from my doctor, I avoided regular checkups. I wasn't completely immune from insulin reactions, but I was able to concentrate on work without having to worry over the particulars of keeping tight control of my diabetes. It takes time and attention to maintain good control of diabetes and I didn't feel I could spare the time or the energy that good control would take away from work.

I had no shortage of excuses and rationalizations to justify my poor control of my diabetes. Eventually, though, my misgivings began to wear away at my façade of indifference and nonchalance. Years of worrying finally brought me around to the point where I was able to admit to myself that by permitting work to dominate my thinking and my priorities, I had developed a distorted and foolish view about my health. This realization was one of the chief factors behind the change in my overall attitude toward work.

Five years ago I took a big step in a different direction in my life as I began to reestablish tight control over my diabetes. There is no magic bullet for controlling diabetes;

no panacea to cure it. Discipline and dedication are required each and every day—close monitoring of blood sugar levels, regular exercise, management of stress, and a strict diet, among many other things needed to keep my metabolism in balance. To maintain good control over my diabetes, I had to remake my whole way of life.

Tightly controlling my diabetes takes time, and at first I was apprehensive that my work might suffer as a result. But to my surprise and delight there has been no detrimental impact on either my performance or my success. Instead, by improving my health I've boosted my energy and rejuvenated my enthusiasm for my job, in no small part because I am no longer haunted by a deep, dark, unsettling fear that work is, literally, killing me.

It seems to me that what I do to manage my diabetes is a microcosm of what's involved in the bigger challenge of balancing life and work—both tasks are complicated, both take time, energy, and attention, both are day to day struggles that must be begun anew each morning, and both require remaking one's way of life. Everything involved in maintaining balance is well worth the effort, though, for in doing what's required one becomes rooted ever more firmly and ever more deeply in the rich, lush complexity and finery of life.

My own efforts at creating balance have been further rewarded, for I have come out on the other side of my fixation on work free of the jaded, disaffected cynicism and disappointment that plague many heavy business travelers. I have been able to reinvigorate my interest in work because balance has made my work better in the same way that balance has improved my life. When work is its own reward, it's not fulfilling, much less a calling, because at this extreme there's no purpose to work other than the work itself. Balance has reconnected me with the kind of work I set out to do when I began my career.

I have seen first-hand that life is not work and work is not life, and from that I have learned that only a life in balance is truly a life in full.

—*J. Walker Smith*

1
A RENAISSANCE LIFE

Every now and then go away, have a little relaxation, since to remain constantly at work will cause you to lose power of judgment. Go some distance away because a lack of harmony or proportion is more readily seen. —Leonardo da Vinci

Such wise advice this is—from Leonardo da Vinci no less, the prodigious polymath of the Italian Renaissance. Painter, sculptor, engineer, astronomer, anatomist, biologist, geologist, physicist, architect, philosopher, humanist. His legacy of work inspires us yet today. Did he ever rest? Well, he certainly believed that balance, too, is a supreme accomplishment, if not the most sublime. This archetypal Renaissance man believed that work suffers, indeed, is inharmonious and out of all proportion, if not tempered by some distance and relaxation. The genius of da Vinci's counsel is not simply that work should be paralleled by life, but rather that without a life, work itself is compromised.

BALANCE—JWS

2
WORK AND EGGS

I enjoy myself most when I am so at peace that activity is secondary. I also know how difficult it is to develop this as habit.—M. C. Richards

The seventeen Trappist monks who live in a monastery at Snowmass, Colorado supported themselves at one time by raising chickens. They also ate eggs, lots of eggs—twenty-seven eggs a week. When researchers came to check their cholesterol, they were shocked to discover that no one had a count of over 130. How was this possible? I have been with several of the monks at conferences. Their life is not simply work. These monks spend hours in centering prayer. Their life has a balance of activity and rest, reflection and prayer, work and play, service and praise. Their spirits have found their center in the Spirit. And so they eat eggs!

BALANCE—RKJ

3

A BREATH OF EVERYTHING

Truly to sing, that is a different breath. A breath to nothing,
a wafting in God. A wind.—Rainer Maria Rilke

The central image in the Academy Award-winning film *American Beauty* is a plastic bag being suspended in the air by the wind, which is captured on video by a teenage boy named Ricky. The image is meant to be a parable for the Spirit that energizes and enriches all of life. For just as the Hebrew word ru'ach means both "wind" and "spirit," so Ricky finds in the prolonged flight of the bag a beauty that is deeply spiritual. He tells his girlfriend Jane that he now realizes there is an entire life behind things. And he believes that this benevolent force wants him to know there is no reason to be afraid.

As in this movie, where Jane's parents let their obsessions with marketing and real estate deafen them to life's real singing, we, too, often fail to recognize the Spirit at work in us. The plastic bag suggests a different breath, a breath for nothing and yet for everything.   BALANCE—RKJ

4

WORK, TENNIS, AND FAMILY

Inner happiness, external play, objective vocational success, mature inner defenses, good outward marriage, all correlate highly—not perfectly, but at least as powerfully as height correlates with weight.—George Vaillant

Several hundred Harvard graduates were studied by Vaillant over a forty-year period in an attempt to understand "the kind of people who do well and are well." His conclusion: being a good businessman (there were no women at Harvard at the time) goes hand in hand with being a good tennis player and husband. Contrary to common mythology, the very men who enjoyed the best marriages and the richest friendships tended also to become the company presidents. BALANCE—RKJ

5

SLEEP IN

With people now waking up to the fact that widespread sleep deprivation is a major threat to our public health and productivity, the ability to get adequate rest has become a new denominator of luxury, status, and privilege.

When was the last time you slept to your heart's content? What would you give for the time off to sleep in? The fresh face of a good night's rest is today's look of success. Eight hours of sleep are harder to come by than a luxury car or a big house. What is it that we think we get more of by sleeping less? Work to the point of exhaustion makes us prone to mistakes as well as less productive. We've become like the Red Queen in Wonderland who tells Alice she is running as fast as she can just to stay in place. Instead, as writer Edward Helmore suggests, we should emulate someone like Albert Einstein who needed ten hours of sleep a night while he was working out the revolutionary concepts of quantum physics and space/time relativity.   BALANCE—JWS

6

CONSTANT MOTION

It was Einstein who made the real trouble. He announced in 1905 that there was no such thing as absolute rest. After that there never was.—Stephen Leacock

The Protestant work ethic is a deep current in America. But even this ethic has always recognized a day of rest. We've almost forgotten this though. Before Einstein's theory of relativity, we never really knew that everything in the universe is in constant motion; nothing truly at rest. But having learned it, this theory has provided a convenient metaphor for our own lives that legitimizes the suffocation of rest by the constant motion of work. Indeed, in no small way, the twentieth century was defined by work: Industrialization. Unions. Rosie the Riveter. What's good for General Motors. *The Organization Man.* Working women. Junk bonds. Glass ceilings. Downsizing. Working moms. Day care. Second careers. Second jobs. Road warriors. Family friendly policies. Telecommuting. Job sharing. Dot-coms. 24–7. In the century to come, though, we would do well to remember that part and parcel of our work ethic, not to mention our work performance, is the need to refresh ourselves with a day of rest. Advancing the right to rest is thus nothing less than a renewed commitment to a better work ethic.

BALANCE—JWS

7

THE TOLL OF KINDNESS

The best portion of a good man's life is his little, nameless, unre-membered acts of kindness and of love.—William Wordsworth

A friend from San Francisco often pays the bridge toll not only for himself but also for the car behind him. What a splendid practical joke! As John leaves the tollbooth, not only is he buoyed in spirit by what he has done, but the toll taker and the driver of the next car are as well. John says he is always renewed by this simple act of generosity, because his mind takes a brief vacation from his own problems.

I can't help but wonder how the drivers of the other cars respond. Do they speed up and try to get a look at the "odd" person who just paid their toll? Are they inspired to do something generous for someone else that day? Or do they just shrug it off and never realize that a spontaneous act of kindness could energize them (and others too) on even the most trying of days?

My friend's action reminds me of those occasions when I too have done something generous for others. The gift usually ends up bringing me more pleasure than inconvenience or cost. In fact, the return on investment seems disproportionate—yet I so seldom make the effort.

BALANCE—RKJ

8
GIVING UNTIL IT FEELS GOOD

Seventy-three percent of Americans gave money to charity in 1999, amounting to $190 billion or 2 percent of our national income. In addition, 49 percent volunteered time to civic activities and organizations.

Morris Popes is an eighty-one-year old retired train engineer whose retirement income is only $1700 per month. Interviewed for a story in *Time* magazine, Popes said he gives $3000 a year to his church and at least $500 a year to Atlanta's Food Bank. When asked why he gives, Pope responded that if everyone felt the pleasure he feels from helping others that he felt, they'd give too.

Even Bill and Melinda Gates have realized there is more to life than Microsoft, donating a staggering $22 billion to their foundation. The Gates see life as something of a tripod: family, company, and philanthropy. With billion-dollar grants helping to finance such things as international vaccination and children's health programs, Bill Gates has reflected that the foundation does work that he can feel good about every day. Absolutely.   BALANCE—RKJ

9
STEALING FROM OURSELVES

According to Saint Augustine, idolatry can be described as "mankind tyrannized over by the work of his own hands."

We, both men and women, have created our own mini-empires that demand time and attention—our large houses, our boats, our cars, our travel, our book groups, our season tickets. Such externals, while good in themselves, pirate our lives when added together. Our busy schedules and material expectations consume our energy, focus our imagination, and dry our spirits. Perhaps things are beginning to change. Polls conducted by Yankelovich show us that owning an expensive car is becoming less important for a growing percentage. But most of us have a long way to go.

It was not until I took a sabbatical from teaching and went with my wife to a small town in Spain that I realized how trapped I had become by the life I had created for myself. Removed from my normal, everyday obligations, I could work eight hours a day and still have eight hours for enjoying my spouse, exploring the town, walking along the beach, reading fiction, cooking new foods, talking with friends, playing tennis, and on and on. Life has a richness far beyond what any of us can produce. It is more a gift to be enjoyed than a task to be managed.

BALANCE—RKJ

10

STRIKING A CHORD

Music will help to dissolve your perplexities and purify your character and sensibility.—Dietrich Bonhoeffer

Bonhoeffer believed that even in times of sorrow and adversity, music had the ability to keep one aware of the gift of life. Churches have long been aware of music's power to convey this deep-based sense of joy. To those absent from our churches, it might be the songs of another Madonna that revitalize the listener. But music's ability to renew hope and bring joy should not be dismissed easily.

Music helps us find the grace in the ordinary. People fill concert halls and rock stadiums for this reason. Last Sunday, as I sat in church and sang along with a group of guitars plus a flute scattering out high notes at a dizzying pace, I again found myself thankful to God for my life. Why? I can't fully say. My schedule remains too hectic, and I don't understand how all that has happened to me fits together. But the music puts me in touch with life at some more central region, and it is transformative.   BALANCE—RKJ

11

THE SEVENTH DAY

T. S. Eliot speaks of the wild thyme and the waterfall, of music that is heard so deeply that the listener is one with the music while the music lasts. For him, these revelations of life's mystery and meaning are partial; they are only hints. But they are hints!

Life is more than music and waterfall, but one might say here its meaning often becomes transparent. Recall the story of the Israelites wandering in the wilderness. When they complained to God that they were without food, he gave them quail for meat and manna from which they could make bread. And the Israelites worked hard at collecting this food. But God also told them that they should only work at gathering their food six days of the week. On the seventh, the sabbath, they were to rest, lest they forget that the food was there because of God's provision and not simply because of their effort. On the sabbath, they were to experience music and the waterfall.

The lesson is a perpetual one. We need the waterfall and the music for the hints they give. They are reminders that we master life by more than the work of our own efforts.

12

JOIN THE DANCE

*In one of Charles Schulz's Peanuts comic strips,
Snoopy is pictured dancing alone. When Lucy joins in,
Snoopy exclaims, "To dance is to live."*

Have you ever gone on a vacation alone? It can be wonderful for the first few days, but soon you want to share your new experiences with someone else, even if a stranger. My wife Cathy and I took a ferry to Tallin, Estonia, one summer. When another American, who had been traveling alone for three weeks, spotted us, he could not wait to talk. The conversation continued long after my wife and I were finished, for he had so much stored up that he wanted to say.

It can be exhilarating to hike alone in the foothills. It is fun to win sitting alone at a computer game. But our experiences of play are best when communal. In coming together by dancing with another, by sharing in silence the beauty of a sunset, by going to a movie together, by playing cards, or even by letting someone watch you play solitaire, joy is elevated to another level.   BALANCE—RKJ

13

A 29.8-HOUR DAY

In a national survey commissioned by MTV Networks/Viacom, people reported on the extent to which they juggle several entertainment and media options at once. When you add it all up, we're doing 5.8 more hours of activities than there are hours in the day! The net result of such multitasking is a 24-hour day crammed with 29.8 hours of stuff to do.

When I was growing up, my sister would gab on her Princess phone with a textbook open beside her, listening to her 45's and following the action on her favorite TV show with the sound turned down. Today my nieces gossip on their cell phones while watching music videos on cable, paging one another and chatting online, with several computer windows simultaneously opened onto a variety of applications and Web sites. The difference between then and now is only a matter of degree. And it's a difference rooted less in the technologies themselves than in the proliferating number of things to do.

We're awash in an unprecedented glut of pastimes and diversions, and we want to do them all. The only way to do them all is to master the ability to do several at once. As a result, we find ourselves living each day filled to overflowing. Should we fret about this? Is it worrisome that we try to beat the clock by doubling and tripling up, piling one thing on top of another in every moment of the day? Multitasking is nothing but a life skill, neither good nor bad in and of itself. Indeed, in the information-saturated future, it's good that our children will be smarter, more efficient processors of knowledge and information. But if multitasking tempts us, and our children, to cross the line and gorge ourselves in a gluttony of distractions, then our challenge will not be keeping technology at bay so much as controlling our overuse of technology by curbing our appetite for ever more diversions. BALANCE—JWS

14

STEP OFF THE GAS

Traffic engineer Walter Kulash likes to remind those who ask for his advice that when it comes to roads and streets, the ones we seem to enjoy the most are those many planners would grade an F, signifying a plan or a design that fails to move traffic as fast as possible. He reminds us that the cities where we like to vacation, such as New Orleans, San Francisco, Santa Fe, or Boston, all have thriving, vibrant, lively communities wherever the street designs work to slow traffic down.

Walter Kulash isn't suggesting that we leave our streets in disrepair. Rather, he's arguing that we should make our streets friendlier. And he has some ideas about how to do so, ideas that cut against the grain of conventional wisdom in urban planning. Kulash says, where possible, slow traffic down. By orthodox criteria, this is a failing level of service, because traditional standards define "better" as faster not slower. But Kulash and other iconoclastic, visionary planners like him relish that failing grade. They believe that if street design is about nothing but the speed and efficiency of traffic flow, communities wind up out of balance, and then feel far worse to the people who live there. There is too much emphasis on the coming and the going, and too little on the being there. Balance is the priority they champion, which means that even if most of the time you design for maximum speed, a lot of the time you should intentionally fail to design for maximum speed. As Kulash likes to remind us, it's not as if we find "failing" levels of traffic service unpalatable per se because, after all, that's what we enjoy on vacation.

The parallel with our personal lives is obvious. Communally and personally, every now and then we need to design a little bottleneck into our plans. BALANCE—JWS

15
TOO MUCH OF A GOOD THING

I have long been of the opinion that if work were such a splendid thing the rich would have kept more of it for themselves.—Bruce Grocott

Of course, if work was really that bad, everybody, rich and poor, would be on strike. Work itself is not the problem; it's work without balance that's the problem. And by creating a balance between work and life, every one of us can own an equal share of the riches.

A friend from graduate school, Bob, started a business shortly after we graduated that quickly became a booming success. With fierce dedication and competitiveness, Bob worked nonstop at building his company. Long active and involved in lots of sports and outdoor activities, Bob gave it all up to put in long hours at the office. But his blood, sweat, and tears at work soon paid off. Several years in a row his business was one of the fastest growing companies of its type in America. When he finally sold his business to an international conglomerate he made tens of millions.

At that point, Bob went from one extreme to the other—he quit working entirely and threw himself nonstop into his favorite sports of tennis, volleyball, hiking, mountain biking, and running. In almost no time, though, to the surprise of everyone who knew him, Bob was back in the office part-time. He explained to me one afternoon that the joy these sports activities had once brought him as a diversion and pastime wasn't there when he took them up as a replacement for work. Sports had become just another job. Bob said he'd come to see that work was important to him, although he realized that he'd lost that feeling for work when he was totally immersed in it just as he'd lost that feeling for his favorite sports in the same way. Bob now understood that he needed balance—not one thing instead of the other. Living a life filled with nothing but leisure had made him no happier than he'd been when he was living a life filled with nothing but work.

Bob told me that he'd always viewed work as a necessary evil—something to be endured unless it could be excised. By viewing work in this way, Bob reflected, he'd created a work environment for himself that he couldn't wait to exit. Only because of his unique chance to live life at the other extreme had Bob come to see that work is an essential part of a balanced life, so long as work itself is kept in balance. Bob concluded that he could have had the satisfactions of balance long before he'd made his millions if only he'd had the wisdom to invest a bit of his time and talents into his life as well as into his work. And, Bob rued, those lost years were a treasure that no amount of money could ever buy back. BALANCE—JWS

16

ALWAYS ON THE CLOCK

Remember that time is money.—Benjamin Franklin

Some of us have grown up with such a belief structure. Just look at our calendars: 7:00 A.M. breakfast meetings; lunch in; three too many appointments for the afternoon; e-mails left for the evening at home. Life has been reduced to the clock. Sometimes the deadlines pile up, so we quite literally "work 'til we drop." But what happens to beauty, wonder, and imagination? Last night when I was driving home at 7:30 P.M., a full moon surprised me as I turned a corner. It was very low on the horizon and dominated the street with its light. It was magical. Thankfully, life is more than our calendars—and time is more than money.

TIME—RKJ

17
NATURE ABHORS A VACUUM

Parents in a Minneapolis suburb are trying to start a national movement to relax children's schedules by asking youth leaders to cut back on group activities and demands so that families can have more time to spend together.

Every week, I spend part of an afternoon looking through my business calendar to see what's looming ahead. Days filled with nothing but big, empty white spaces rouse in me a compulsion to get busy and ink them in with things to do. I get antsy not knowing for sure that every day is going to be packed full. It's a craving to fill in the blanks, and I have to fight it like an addiction because I know how bad it can be for me.

I once put myself underwater for the better part of a year with back-to-back-to-back meetings, sales calls, interviews, presentations, speeches, deadlines, and travel. All I did was run around. With little time to think or prepare, my work suffered. The best I could do was whatever I could get done at the last minute, which wasn't as good as it could have been. So I've had to change. Now I try to leave time open in my schedule to rest and catch up, to absorb and reflect. But this is not easy to stick with because the pressure to overschedule is unrelenting. We all know what this is like. We live full lives, busy with purpose and activity, in which we try to make every second count. We're reminded constantly that time is slipping away, so we're anxious to put every moment to good use.

Yet, even as we assert control, we lose it. Why? Because the calendar takes over. Planners and organizers need lots of things to plan and organize. It's easy to give into the temptation to add more and more until all the slots are filled in. Having done it, we then take satisfaction in how good it all looks on paper. But quite often this is a hollow satisfaction, for the things that get squeezed out by an overfull calendar are often the very things we're trying to cultivate and support by squeezing in so much. Too much is lost by trying to do too much. As I have found in my work, easing off is the first step toward recovery of what we most want.

18

THE RICHES OF TIME

Anthropologists studying the Machiguenga Indians of Peru found that these traditional hunters and gatherers actually have four more hours of free time a day than their contemporaries in more advanced twentieth-century societies. Plus, the Machiguenga's pace of life is more relaxed and less stressful.

In a world where everyone and everything tries to move at Internet speed, deciding how to define affluence is not just a rhetorical exercise. This research about the Machiguenga Indians of Peru was first published in 1978 in the professional journal *Human Nature* under the title, "In Search of the Affluent Society." Modern societies produce more stuff to buy but less free time. If affluence were measured by time, not by stuff, then modern life would be viewed as more, not less, impoverished.

I love to read poetry. My favorite poets are A. R. Ammons, Mary Oliver, Czeslaw Milosz, Seamus Heaney, Billy Collins, Mark Strand, Robert Morgan, May Swenson, Mark Doty, John Ashberry, Elizabeth Bishop, Kenneth Rexroth, Michael McFee, Rodney Jones, e. e. Cummings, Gary Snyder, Emily Dickinson, W. H. Auden, Walt Whitman, James Merrill, Wallace Stevens, and William Butler Yeats. Reading good poetry takes time. To really appreciate it, I need time to study it carefully, recite it aloud, and absorb the meanings, nuances, and subtleties. With my business travel schedule, it's hard to find the time it takes to read good poetry. But irrespective of how much business I generate when I travel for work, I feel my life is diminished and impoverished in some way whenever my travel prevents me from being able to take the time I need to read good poetry.

So I am trying to enrich my travel and my life by diligently setting aside an hour to read poetry each night I stay in a hotel on a business trip. I carry a volume with me when I travel and no matter what I have to do or what I need to prepare, I make a point to read poetry for an hour every night I'm on the road. It means that my business travel is not only time spent on work, it's also the time I have built into my life to read good poetry. I can look forward to traveling because it means I'll be reading poetry. This makes business travel less of a chore and more of a treat, and hence an experience that compensates me in a far richer fashion.

TIME—JWS

19

TIME-SAVING GADGETS

In fact, I think I should not go far wrong if I asserted that the amount of genuine leisure available in a society is generally in inverse proportion to the amount of labor-saving machinery it employs.—E. F. Schumacher

By some estimates, the average American will work one month longer than he or she worked just twenty years ago. When the increase in two-income families is also factored in, the picture is even bleaker. With our extra money (or more plastic), we buy more gadgets in the hope of saving more time—trash compactors, electronic organizers, gas grills and gas logs in fireplaces, pants pressers, timed sprinklers. Yet we have less time. The equation never seems quite to work.

If Schumacher is correct, perhaps we need to stop depending on so many labor-saving devices. Building a fire in the fireplace brings real satisfaction and causes one to pause to enjoy the fire. Watering the flower pots in the back yard allows one to again enjoy one's garden. Even taking the garbage outside to the trash barrels can be the occasion to pause and enjoy the distant mountains. Leisure comes in many guises, but it happens only as we slow down to enjoy again the life that is ours.   TIME—RKJ

20
TO DO NOTHING

The measure of a person is how they handle their time alone.

The psychiatrist Carl Jung is reported to have counseled an overworked minister who came to him for help. Jung listened to his story and then instructed him to do nothing each day for two hours. When the pastor returned for his next appointment, he told Jung how wonderful it had been to listen to Mozart each day. Jung replied, "I told you to do nothing. I didn't want you even to listen to music." "Oh," responded the minister, "I couldn't stand to be alone with myself for that long." "Think of how the members of your church must feel each Sunday," said Jung.   TIME—RKJ

21
SAVING MY BUMPER

A health study sponsored by World Bank found that business travelers are three times as likely as non-travelers to file insurance claims for treatment of the stress, worry, and depression that comes from being on the road.

I flew in once from a long business trip. The line to pay for parking was very slow, which began to rekindle my frustrations from the week just past. So when I heard the cashier tell the driver ahead of me she would have to call in for approval of the check, I lost it. Who pays for airport parking with a check?! This was too much. Just then a new lane opened, so I threw the car into reverse and gunned it to get over there. But I had cut the wheel too sharply, and abruptly my car jumped sideways as I rebounded off the abutment in front of the cashier, who was now staring at me and the front of my car with saucer-sized eyes and a hand over her mouth. But as an A team business traveler with an image to maintain, I wasn't about to let a little dent stop me. I'd show them. I man-handled the car to the other lane, paid, and sped off. I'd worry about the damage later. But the steering quickly became sluggish, so I moved to the right to let a silver van pass and saw in its reflection that my front bumper was folded up almost completely underneath my car. This made me madder. I swerved over, stopped in the break-down lane and wrenched the bumper out. It had been hanging on by a mere sliver of plastic, which snapped off as I held the bumper. Yet madder still, I wedged the bumper into the back seat and raced home, weaving in and out of traffic with a skeletal grille and dangling wires sparking on the asphalt. At home, as I dumped the bumper in the backyard, I caught my wife's eye through the kitchen window. Without a trace of a surprise, she shook her head at me and went back to cooking dinner.

It was one of those moments when you get an image of yourself that's not pretty. What had the last hour been about? So when I read that the World Bank had found, in a follow-up study to the one mentioned above, that typically business travelers are unlikely to take the time they need to rest up once they get home from a long, tiring trip, I didn't spout any of my old sarcasm about weaklings who needed rest. Instead, I saw a metaphorical parallel from my own life, that of dumping the bumpers we smash up at work, often for no good reason at all, in our own backyards—and that without rest and decompression, our lives may hang in the balance by nothing more a thin sliver of plastic. Now I make a point to pause and catch my breath, so I can save my bumper for when I'll really need it.

WORK—JWS

22

KEEPING UP

There is more to life than merely increasing its speed.—Gandhi

Harvard President Neil Rudenstine found himself unable to get up one morning in November 1994. In the midst of a huge fund-raising campaign and assaulted by more work than he could process day after day, he had tried to run faster and faster until he finally collapsed. "Exhausted" was the headline banner on the cover of the *Newsweek* magazine that chronicled his plight. It took a three-month sabbatical—listening to Ravel, walking with his wife on the beach, reading—before Rudenstine could return to his work.

Many of us can identify with Rudenstine. We too are being forced to increase our speed in order to keep up. We are overwhelmed and overworked, and the result is the same as it was for Rudenstine—a feeling of exhaustion. We need to find our rest. We might not get the gift of a sabbatical, but little "sabbaths" along the way can help restore and renew.

WORK—RKJ

23

A LARGER CALLING

Everyone has a vocation by which he earns his living, but
he also has a vocation in an older sense of the word—
the vocation to use his powers and live his life well.
—Richard W. Livingstone

The word "vocation" comes from the Latin noun, "voca-tio," meaning summons, and behind this from the Latin verb "vocare," to call. Many of us equate our sense of vocation, or calling, with our work. But it is more than this. It was Martin Luther who argued that the work of the common person could have spiritual value, just as much as that of the priest. For Luther, our vocation was to serve God as a craftsman or milkmaid. Our "vocation" is not simply that of being a worker. Rather, our work is a response to some larger calling.

The difference is subtle, but profound. One approach to the workplace is constricting; the other, expansive. One, isolating; the other, community building. The mailroom attendant at my work could simply collect packages and give stamps. Instead, she engages each of us in conversation and ends up brightening our day. She would have her deep sense of gladness toward life be contagious. As individuals and as a society, we need to recover such a sense of work as a calling, to use that sense of work as part of our powers to make life better.

WORK—RKJ

24

THE END OF THE ROAD

Therapists who have worked with high-level executives are used to their promises of cutting back on travel. However, these psychiatrists know that these business people are just fooling themselves because in reality they are addicted to travel; they just can't stop.

I'm on the road for business so much that staying at home for any extended period of time feels like stepping off the space shuttle after a month in orbit. At the end of one year not too long ago, I did not get on a plane or take a cab or sleep in a hotel room between Thanksgiving and New Year's. It was eerie. I distinctly remember one afternoon when I felt my pulse slow and settle at a lower rate. I found I couldn't go near malls that holiday season because I was suddenly allergic to the clamor and aggressiveness and hectic pace. Some afternoons, I was content to do nothing but stare out the window at my backyard. When I finally went back out on the road again, I discovered to my amazement that I had missed the airport! It occurred to me then that the airport is where I go to work. It's the place I know and the place that electrifies me. I had to admit to myself that like it or not, I get cravings for the road. By coming to understand this about myself, I am able now to find a better balance of work in my life. There is, indeed, a place for how I work and what I do. Getting completely away from work isn't any more satisfying than giving myself completely over to work. So while it may seem like I'm addicted to the road, in fact what I'm addicted to is life. Part of my life, although certainly not the whole of it, is work. So these days I try to sustain a balance between work and life, not try to escape one for the other. WORK—JWS

25

IN THE BLACK, AND BLUE

A recent review of research around the world found that basically no correlation between income and happiness exists in advanced countries, which is to say, being rich doesn't make a person happier.

This is bad news if you've grown too used to blaming your blues on your paycheck. But it's great news otherwise. It proves that, indeed, the pursuit of happiness is an inalienable right not subject to the whims of either government or the market. Ironically, though, this news is so good that it puts our happiness at risk. In chasing the almighty dollar, we Americans don't realize that accumulating more and more won't make us happier and happier. And from this emerges the paradox of the recent boom economy: even as we had more money than ever before, study after study found we were no happier than before and, quite often, unhappier.

Research to the contrary notwithstanding, we expect more money to bring greater happiness. Not finding it makes us that much more frustrated and unhappy. Because even when we get there financially, we still don't feel as if we've arrived. The difficulty is that we can't write a check for happiness. For happiness, we have to look to our lives not to our checkbooks. We have all we need to afford a king's ransom of happiness.

WORK—JWS

26
THE LONGEST SHORT KISS

God is interested in a lot of things besides religion. God is the Lord and Creator of all life, and there are manifestations of the holy in its celebration or in its repudiation—in every aspect of the common life.—Joseph Sittler

Have you seen *Fantasia 2000*? Here is a movie that will buoy your spirits and bring a smile to young and old alike. Tim Allen, a friend who worked as an animator on the project, spent a month or more drawing Donald and Daisy's final kiss at the end of the "Pomp and Circumstance" selection. Why would someone spend so much time working on these drawings that lasted only seconds on screen and whose only purpose is to entertain? Surely so God might smile too.

WORK—RKJ

27

WHAT'S AN 8-HOUR DAY?

In 1998 Americans worked four and one-half half weeks longer than they did the decade before. This added time at work accounts for almost three-quarters of the typical family's gain in income over that period of time.

More and more people, close to 20 percent in 1999, are choosing to work overtime hours to maintain their standard of living. In fact, the preservation of overtime pay was a key issue in the bitter strike of Los Angeles bus drivers in the fall of 2000. Although their income was already more than the typical schoolteacher, they still wanted the option to earn more by working more.

When the eight-hours-a-day movement was begun by labor 130 years ago, the purpose was to limit the work day, to give workers a life outside their job. In France, it is even illegal for workers to work more than 39 hours a week.

But in the United States, times have changed. Now workers are using the forty-hour week to increase their overtime pay, competing with colleagues to get a bigger share of the extended hours.

Rather than scaling back as incomes have become stagnant, people are making up for it by working overtime or taking second jobs. We no longer are trying to keep up with the Joneses. We are working to keep up with ourselves. What hangs in the balance is the quality of our lives.

WORK—RKJ

28

IN PLAIN VIEW

At one point in the early seventies David Merrick, the Broadway producer, shared with a friend how he felt about his enormous success. Merrick compared it to mountain climbing where you struggle to make the summit, even having lives lost along the way, but at the top all you discover is "snow and ice."

David Merrick is one of the storied figures in the history of the Broadway stage. He brought us one joyous hit after another during his long career—*Fanny, Gypsy, Hello Dolly!, Promises, Promises, 42nd Street,* even *The Great Gatsby* on the silver screen. Yet, for Merrick, all of this came with a somber footnote. We're not unfamiliar with his feeling, for on occasion we've all been through this sort of big let-down at the end of a tough climb, no matter how successful. But most of us come to realize something else too—that the most fulfilling satisfactions and rewards are not isolated atop out-of-the-way peaks that lie at the limits of our reach and endurance but, rather, are to be found in the hike itself. As long as we proceed with a pace and a purpose for taking in the views along the way, it's a hike that's truly satisfying however high we climb. Of course, this sounds too obvious to bear repeating, until we see that sometimes even the most accomplished among us never discover this very ordinary secret to life's most extraordinary rewards.   WORK—JWS

29
COMING BACK TO LIFE

March 14: I felt like I'd waited all my life to peel off my city ways, city life, and get into the woods. If you let it be, if you forget old things, and learn new ones, even a week can last forever.—Rick Bass

As a young couple, writer Rick Bass and his wife, artist Elizabeth Hughes, moved to the wilds of Montana's Yaak Valley to pioneer a new home for themselves. Bass wrote of that transforming experience in his book *Winter.* Bass chronicled that first winter as a diary of backbreaking labor, although tempered most days with unexpected discoveries of breathtaking beauty. Their fortitude that winter paid off. For they didn't just make it through, they came back to life. When was the last time you worked hard at something that animated you so much you felt you'd live forever?

WORK—JWS

30

DISCOVERING THE DANCE

The splendor of dance is when you trust and enjoy.
—Mai, in the movie, Shall We Dance?.

The Japanese movie *Shall We Dance?* portrays a white-collar worker, Shohei Sogiyama, who married at twenty, became a father at thirty, and bought a house with a garden at forty. Pretty good for Tokyo (or for San Francisco)! Dedicated to his work, Sogiyama leaves early in the morning and comes home late. He knows he should be happier with his life, but he is not—until, that is, he discovers ballroom dancing! You might smile. When I saw the movie with a theater full of Japanese, they were falling out of their chairs laughing over the incongruity of it all: Japanese businessmen simply don't go to ballroom dancing classes. But the audience also cheered Sogiyama on.

We all need those opportunities to step out of character. Rosie Grier knits. Madonna reads the kabbalah. Sylvester Stallone paints. Gwyneth Paltrow loves yoga. Paul Newman cooks. Harry and Bess Truman watched professional wrestling. Jay Leno has his motorcycles and Sarah Michelle Gellar bowls. There is a lot more to life than just a single role to play. LIVING—RKJ

31

SIMPLE SATISFACTIONS

According to nationwide surveys conducted by Yankelovich, 60% of GenXers are trying to turn their wishes for a simpler lifestyle into reality, while 59% of baby boomers regret never having done so.

My wife Cathy and I spent a week one summer in Sweden on the island of Gotland. Visby is a beautiful medieval walled city that overlooks a calm sea. Its cobblestoned streets and manicured parks are a delight. We stayed in a simple cabin, rode bicycles into the countryside, explored the town by looking at architecture, shops, and art, read on the beach, slept, ate, and talked. Our expectations were nothing in particular. We had no schedule. Yet our days became filled with small pleasures, and the outcome was refreshment and renewal.

Each evening we would walk to the town square and sit outside at a small restaurant next to the ruins of an old church. Cathy and I would reflect on the day, watching the sky go black. Then we would eat a wonderful Swedish meal while gazing at times in reverie at the colored illuminations on the crumbling cathedral. It was nothing special, I guess, but for us, it seemed priceless. LIVING—RKJ

32

A REVERENT RHYTHM

Fishing is as much a religion as a sport.—Izaak Walton

Speak to anyone who fly-fishes and he or she will describe the experience with almost a reverence. Even ice fishing has its devotees. The movie *A River Runs Through It* will help those of us who do not fish to understand its lure. Those who fish like the solitude even though, ironically enough, they are not really alone. Standing in the middle of the stream, they feel connected with something larger than themselves. Casting and reeling and casting again, the rhythm allows them to lose themselves in the majesty of the world around them. Distance runners talk of the same sensation. So too do those who practice centering prayer. Some even speak of "catching the universe." We all need those occasions of transcendence, of solitary immersion, to give life its context and its meaning.

LIVING—RKJ

33

MY FRONT PORCH

In a national poll conducted by Yankelovich, 60 percent of Americans said their current neighborhood was as friendly or friendlier than the neighborhood in which they grew up.

My back porch is a serene spot overlooking an overgrown, wooded gully that buffers us from the clamor and commotion of the metropolis in which we live. The view is lush with hundred foot trees, flowering vines, scurrying wildlife, scores of birds, even the occasional hawk. On cool, misty fall mornings, my back porch feels like a secret mountain hideaway. In contrast, my front porch is not hidden away at all. It's wide open to the street. Sitting there on a rocker or the porch swing, I feel connected to all the neighborhood goings-on. Neighbors come up to talk. The mail carrier waves. Children scamper by. Strolling couples nod hello as their dogs trot over for a pat on the head. I watch deliverymen drop off packages and yardmen put the finishing touches on lawns. Up and down the block, life spills out, and on my front porch, I feel caught up in it.

More and more, my front porch is where I sit. I used to crave the solitude in the back, but over time I began to feel as if I was slowly subsiding from life, sinking inward. I've come to understand that what I need most is the community out front; it buoys me up as it sweeps me along in its current. It's enlivening and animating, and as friendly and as nourishing as I'm willing to make it. I still need my back porch as an occasional getaway, but on my front porch I feel so invigorated by life that I don't want to let any of it get away from me. LIVING—JWS

34
A FAMILY AWAKENING

Surveys show that the number of breakfasts carried from home has doubled since 1984 and that the number of people eating a fast-food breakfast has gone up 28 percent since 1995.

Ten percent of us begin our commuting between 5:00 A.M. and 6:00 A.M. To beat the traffic, we skip eating at home. Many companies now even serve breakfast to their employees. With our work demanding longer hours, increased productivity, and lengthier commutes, more and more of us arrive early to the workplace to sort through e-mail and get a jump on the day. What is lost in the race, however, is that extra time with family.

When my girls were small, I negotiated with my boss to work at home two to three afternoons a week so that I could be present for my kids. I was not there when they woke up in the morning, but I was there when they got up from their naps. Some of my work had to move into the late evening hours, but the time with Liz and Margi more than made up for less sleep.

LIVING—RKJ

35

DOUBLE DUTY

*Air Force pilots have always prided themselves on their
dedication and commitment to the service, which often
left family at the bottom of the priority list. But now
there are hints and reports of an important cultural
change among young fliers, a new generation of pilots no
longer willing to take it for granted that family always
comes second to work.*

How safe do we feel with a fighting force that puts family
first? Do we feel any less secure to hear that pilots are having second thoughts about what they're willing to sacrifice
for their country? Just who wears the jumpsuit in these
families anyway? There's something new in the air—top
guns leaving behind their derring-do for diaper duty.

It is now time for those in uniform to earn their stripes
in their own backyards, for balancing life and work is no
less a struggle for servicemen than for civilians. Everyone
wants something more. And our national security is better
defended when both our borders and our families are sta-

ble and secure. As much as we need pilots patrolling the wild blue yonder, so too do we need pilots with their feet on the ground, men and women who understand that the point of it all is the life lived way down here, not the work done way up there. Flying under fire takes nerve, courage, quick reflexes, and creativity. So does family. It's the home front as much as the battlefront where this kind of fiber and fortitude needs to be deployed nowadays.   LIVING—JWS

36
PUTTING DOWN STAKES

In a nationwide survey commissioned by the New York Times, 61 percent of respondents agreed that America was better when people had stronger attachments to their communities and didn't relocate from town to town as much.

I know lots of executives who have moved lots of times, including one CEO who has moved ten times in the last twelve years. That's a bit extreme, perhaps, but not particularly rare. However, every person I know who has moved a lot eventually reaches a point where he or she stops moving. And then they live like me. Years ago, I put down stakes and let it be known that it would take more than a new job to get me to move again. I wanted a place where I could feel a connection. Even more, I wanted a place where my family could feel a connection. I knew that moving every few years would be hardest on my family. After all, work would keep me busy and take me to interesting places. But they would be living daily life wherever I took them. A good location was most important for them. Constant relocation would make them feel even more at sea than me. So we settled down in a place we liked. I decided that when work required it, as indeed it has, I'd fly back and forth. My weekends, at least, would be spent where I'd made a home. For me personally it's just small stab at attachment because I still spend a lot of time away. But nevertheless, it gives me a sense of continuity and a place I can point to with my family and say, this is home for us.

LIVING—JWS

37

THE SINCEREST FORM OF FLATTERY

Let him kiss me with the kisses of his mouth!
For your love is better than wine,
your anointing oils are fragrant,
your name is perfume poured out;
therefore the maidens love you.
—Song of Songs 1:2–3 (NRSV)

Such extravagant language! Here is an ancient Hebrew love song in which the woman compliments her beloved. We would use other language today, but the sentiment would be identical. How much fun it is to shower praise on someone you love, to use hyperbole and mean it. Though you might "work" at such flattery, this is not work at all. It's life as it is intended to be lived! Contrary to the old adage, flattery that is meant often accomplishes more than the best of our designs. Here is a model for the family, too, and for the workplace and the neighborhood.   LIVING—RKJ

38

STEPPING OVER PEOPLE

A man was going down from Jerusalem to Jericho, and fell into
the hands of robbers, who stripped him, beat him, and went
away, leaving him half dead.—Luke 10:30 (NRSV)

So begins Jesus' parable of the Good Samaritan. Some years ago, Princeton Seminary reenacted the scenario. They told one group of students that they were to give a speech on job opportunities. The other group read the parable of the Good Samaritan and were told to prepare a talk on it. Students were then sent across campus to the place where their speech was to be recorded. On the way they encountered a confederate who was lying on the street coughing and groaning, pretending to be in pain. Of the forty who passed by, only sixteen stopped to help; twenty-three failed to stop; and one even stepped over the injured man.

Contrary to expectation, the reading of the biblical parable made no difference in who stopped to help. Rather, those who were told ahead of time that they were late to the recording session did not stop; those who were told they could take their time were more likely to stop. What's to be learned? Those of us rushing from one appointment to the next with little black books filled with work appointments are not necessarily bad people, but we will tend to miss opportunities for compassion, friendship and service. We might even step over people. LIVING—RKJ

39

RISKING LIFE

The only equipment we require to live out the image of good-ness in the world is what we have, because God has given us by his very creation of us a capacity to image, to imagine what is good, what is true, and what is beautiful.—Peter Gomes

On my way into a concert hall, I was stopped by a woman coming out of an adjoining theater where she had seen Arthur Miller's *Death of a Salesman*. She explained that she couldn't get home because her car wouldn't start, and she did not have cash or credit cards with her. Could I help her pay for a tow truck? A number of scenarios flashed through my mind, but it did not take any unique capacity to project what I should do. I had the money in my pocket that could solve her problem. I gave her my address so she could mail me a check, wished her well, and handed over the money. She left a little surprised, but grateful. The music had an increased beauty that night. Whether it was actually more glorious, or just that I was prepared to receive it, I am not sure. But goodness and beauty merged naturally in my spirit.

In the movie *Grand Canyon,* an impatient driver takes a wrong turn looking for a shortcut late at night after attending a basketball game and finds himself in a scary neighborhood. When his car develops engine trouble, he begins to panic, and for good reason. Soon a carload of gangbangers approach and things seem bleak. But the tow truck arrives moments later and a conversation ensues between the tow truck driver and the troublemakers. Despite the imminent danger, the tow truck driver simply instructs the scared driver to get in his cab, hooks up the car, and drives away, leaving the gang members speechless. The driver risked his own life and job without considering the options. It was simply the right thing to do.

Sometimes we talk ourselves out of what we know is right, or true, or beautiful. But at other times, we follow the voice within us, and life feels right. Or rather, life is right!

LIVING—RKJ

40
RE-TOLD TALES

In a nationwide survey, three-quarters or more of respondents reported that they "frequently" see aggressive acts of driving like speeding, tailgating, or unsafe maneuvers. A NASA analysis of air flights disrupted by unruly passengers revealed that pilots had to leave the cockpit in four out of ten of those instances, leading to flying errors one-quarter of the times they were forced to do so.

Sometimes it seems no matter where we go or how we get there, our run-ins with other people only fulfill our worst expectations. This has become such a deeply ingrained expectation that it shapes the stories we tell ourselves to guide our lives, most notably, the urban legends we pass on as fact. While not literally true, these urban legends do reveal a truth about us, namely, our sense of what's plausible, even likely, these days. These urban legends ring true to us, hence we believe them. It's the maniac waiting beneath your car in the parking lot to slash your ankles and then rob you. Or the necking couple who hears a radio warning of an escapee from the local asylum with a hook for a hand, so they speed away from lover's lane but once home, find a bloody hook hanging from their car door handle. Or the fruit that explodes in the backseat, splattering the head of the driver who panics and thinks that she's been shot. Or the call that a stolen handbag has been recovered, luring someone away from home so crooks can clean it out. Or the child who disappears in a store, only to be found just in the nick of time, almost unrecognizable after having been given a quick makeover in the bathroom.

All these urban legends tell of nothing except our paranoid expectations about others. What if we told ourselves different stories? Would our expectations change? Would we then be more likely to encounter the better side of people? There is at least one such story. It begins like an urban legend: "A man was going down from Jerusalem to Jericho, and fell into the hands of robbers, who stripped him, beat him, and went away, leaving him half dead." Then, like an urban legend it builds upon our paranoia: "Now by chance a priest was going down that road; and when he saw him, he passed by on the other side. So likewise a Levite." But it concludes much more hopefully: "But a Samaritan while traveling came near him; and when he saw him, he was moved with pity. He went to him and bandaged his wounds, having poured oil and wine on them. Then he put him on his own animal, brought him to an inn, and took care of him." (Luke 10:30–34 *NRSV*)

LIVING—JWS

41
THE BEST MEDICINE

People who laugh actually live longer than those who don't laugh.—James D. Walsh, M.D.

Norman Cousins, writer and editor of *Saturday Review*, beat back a life-threatening disease by adding humor to his therapy. His healing did not come only from the best procedures, medicine, or advice. Rather, Cousins looked past despair for ways to laugh instead—e.g. by watching comedic films—demonstrating through word and action the truth of the old adage, "Laughter is the best medicine."

LIVING—RKJ

42
DAMN LIES & STATISTICS

Researchers have found that laughing is an aerobic workout— oxygen intake is boosted, blood pressure drops, and tension drains away into a deep, sustained relaxation.

I was very much the earnest young know-it-all at my first job out of graduate school. I was convinced that my training in statistics and survey research was going to save American business, starting with this company. To me it was serious stuff, too serious, in fact, for any smiles or chuckles. One day, an anonymously sent cartoon showed up in my in-box. It had been ripped out of a magazine and it depicted a couple leaving a party. The man had an easel under his arm on which a statistical chart was showing. Standing at the door to leave, the woman was reproving him. On the copy of the cartoon sent to me, though, the man's name had been scratched out of her admonishment and my name scribbled in: "Frankly, Walker, you're beginning to bore everyone with your statistics."

It was a pretty clever prank. I tried not to take it personally, even though I'd been singled out by name. Instead, I took it as a lesson that I'd do much better if I lightened up a bit. I believe I've been a lot more successful over the years by applying this lesson to what I do. In business settings I think people are afraid to just let go and laugh because we worry that we won't be taken seriously if we smile too much. But I've found that a good laugh can often melt the frowns that put us on edge and make us more prone to criticizing and arguing with one another for no good reason.

When I give speeches, I always start by making a joke about myself. My speeches are about marketplace trends seen in the research data collected by my firm and I speak to business audiences that are always a little leery of statisticians on stage. So I open my speeches by saying, "I know that the prospect of some Ph.D. researcher standing up here talking about statistics his firm has collected is probably not the sort of thing that got you out of bed this morning with a smile on your face." I pause and go on. "No doubt, you're worrying that I'm going to stand here and use my numbers to torture you for an hour with obscurity and murkiness. But I'm not. I'm not that kind of researcher. When people talk about lies, damn lies, and statistics, I am not the statistics kind of researcher. I'm much more the damn liar kind of guy!"

A good "ha-ha" is the best way to get people ready for an important "ah-ha." And people won't get to the "amen" I'm shooting for at the end of my speeches if they're not nodding "ah-ha" all along the way. A heartfelt chuckle at the start is the best introduction for the serious message to come.

LIVING—JWS

43

TO THINE OWN SELF BE TRUE

We are what we pretend to be, so we must be careful about what we pretend to be.—Kurt Vonnegut

My first Chicago business trip was an overnighter, so a grad school friend insisted I visit her parents there and see the historic old house in which she'd grown up. It sounded like fun. When I got into town her parents told me which train to take to their suburb and said they'd meet me at the station. I left my hotel so early I was able to get on the train before the one they'd told me to take. I figured I'd just get there ahead of schedule and wait. When I got off at my stop, I saw a car across the tracks with an older couple in it staring hard at me. I'd only met her parents once, so I wasn't sure if I recognized this couple. They pointed at me quizzically and I shrugged, which seemed to connect us. We hugged and shook hands. They said they were expecting me on the next train. Ah, I thought, this confirms it. I explained I'd left the hotel early. They said their daughter had talked so highly of me and they recognized me because I was as blonde as she'd said. The only disquieting thing was that the woman kept calling me Mike, which is not my name. But I just thought it must have slipped her mind for a moment. Then they said we should get to the restaurant. Well, that was odd, because they'd said we'd eat at their house, which I'd come to see. But if that's what they wanted to do, it was fine by me.

As we were driving out through the parking lot, the next train was approaching, and just then the man leaned across his wife to remark about someone standing on the platform. I looked over, too, and was so shocked I forgot to breathe for a second or two. There was my friend's father! I recognized him instantly from the one time I'd met him. He was looking down the track at the train pulling in, and here I was in the backseat of a moving car with two strangers! My mind was reeling as the woman turned in the front seat and said to me, "Well, Mike . . ." I sat straight up and said I was sorry, but my name wasn't Mike. The car jerked to a stop. I said I was supposed to meet that other man and I had to go. I closed the door on their stunned faces, then sprinted up behind my friend's father before he could see where I'd come from. I hailed him and he turned to me with surprise. As we spoke, I had a moment of intense, vivid déjà vu as he and I began having the exact conversation I'd just finished: "Weren't you supposed to be on the next train? Our daughter speaks of you so highly. I was looking for your blonde hair." I nodded to everything while slowly coaxing him to his car to make a quick getaway before I'd be forced to confess my mistake. As we drove off, I saw the other couple searching dazedly through the crowd for that other blonde out-of-towner. Dinner that night was an out-of-body experience for me as I struggled not to hyperventilate and faint.

Back home, I told my wife to say nothing, hoping this would go undiscovered. But a week later, my friend phoned, saying she'd just gotten off the phone with her dad. She paused. He'd been to the barber that day. Apparently a casual acquaintance of his was there, too, and had told him about this odd thing that had happened to him at the train station the week before. I was found out! We dissolved into howls of laughter. What I had pretended to be was the picture-perfect visitor, striding gracefully into town full of charm and savoir faire, when in fact I had been any-thing but, bumbling around at the train station like some rube from the sticks. It was just good luck I'd tried to dis-semble with friends, who were only too gleeful to tease me about my pretensions. It was, I've come to see, my penal-ty-free lesson about having the courage to own up to what I don't know, to ask the dumb question when I need to, and to admit to stupid mistakes with a smile.   LIVING—JWS

44

OBSERVE YOUR PLAY

It takes a mature person to play.

Psychologists note that perfectionists don't play with abandon. Loners are eliminated from most games; suspi-cious people don't have fun; and paranoid people are too earnest. If you are self-indulgent or overdependent, you spoil your play. Depressed individuals don't experience pleasure when it is appropriate. If you want a barometer of your normality, don't check your work patterns—observe your play.   PLAY—RKJ

45

A GOOD GAME SPOILED

Al Goss was a pioneering inventor who developed a paging system for doctors in 1949. It failed to catch on. Goss said that the doctors hated his invention because they worried that "it would interrupt their golf games."

The late Al Goss, a recipient of the Lemelson-M.I.T. Lifetime Achievement Award for Invention, developed patents that anticipated numerous wireless inventions from garage-door openers to cell phones. While serving in the O.S.S., he developed a top secret system for spies to transmit information to planes flying overhead. But even he couldn't jump-start a technology like pagers at a time when people preferred to live without them.

When we fret and complain about the technologies of work stalking our lives, we have to remember that it's happening only because we don't seem to mind having our golf games interrupted anymore. If we do mind, we have to say so, which more and more of us are starting to do. But you don't have to totally reject technologies to maintain balance. For example, the chief technology officer of a dot-com company said in a newspaper profile that he is immersed in technologies at work but not at home. He said that he doesn't feel the need to have laptops and cell phones and personal digital assistants at home. He doesn't want technologies to control or enslave his life. For him, technology is just a tool. The wisdom of this is the reminder that our tools don't choose us, we choose them. So we have ultimate control over whether technologies affect our lives for better or for worse. If we say no to technologies, we're not rejecting them so much as containing them and keeping them in proper balance within our lives. PLAY—JWS

46
FUN IF I HAVE TO

That state is a state of slavery in which a man does what he likes to do in his spare time and in his working time that which is required of him.—Eric Gill

What if we were required to go out and have fun? Would we think of it as a chore? Would we look for ways to get around doing it? Would we look for shortcuts? Would we try to hire someone to do it for us? Would we put it off until the last minute? And once we took care of it, what would we do with our time off? Seems kind of silly, doesn't it? Yet more and more, we're squeezing time for fun into whatever time slots are available, which means that once the time for fun has arrived, it's pretty much required that we spend that time having fun. Is this what we mean by fun? Does the scheduling get in the way of having fun?

One of my favorite things to do for fun is to run. To just get out and release myself for an hour. I make a point to avoid pacing myself against other runners, to stay on streets free of cars and construction, and to stop however often I feel like it. If I didn't do these things, then running would be more of the same old competition, stress, and bustle I get at work, and even though I'd still be getting good exercise, I just wouldn't be having any fun. PLAY—JWS

47

THE ART OF THE FRIVOLOUS

We are all of us compelled to read for profit, party for contracts, bowl for unity, drive for mileage, gamble for charity, go out for the evening for the greater glory of the municipality, and stay home for the weekend to rebuild the house.—Walter Kerr

Walter Kerr, a New York drama critic, wrote these words in 1962. But for many, things have not changed much in the intervening years. Too often, we engineer our lives into ever tighter configurations, trying to squeeze out of them every drop of value. Then we wonder why we feel shriveled up. Listen to Kerr again, "In a contrary and perhaps rather cruel way the twentieth century has relieved us of labor without at the same time relieving us of the conviction that only labor is meaningful."

Many of us need to recover the art of the frivolous. What is it we enjoy doing for its own sake? What brings us pleasure without there being any "cash" advantage? Listening to music? Going to movies? Painting? Playing Candyland with our kids? Fixing old cars? Having an aquarium? Cooking? For many of us, there is little danger in going overboard. Instead, such respite from our work agendas will prove useful despite its seeming uselessness. Such is the paradox of play.

PLAY—RKJ

48

POSTED: NO TRESPASSING

Technology and the virtual office have obscured any dividing line between home and office. Genuine leisure—true time off—no longer exists.

Years ago I was in a meeting listening to someone explain a business idea based on her personal observations about the habits of daily business commuters. In the mornings, commuters concentrated on getting ready for the day ahead, sorting through briefs, memos, and reports. In contrast, in the evenings commuters relaxed with a newspaper or a book or a magazine. It was an astute characterization of commuting behaviors, and it shocked me. Why? Because when I thought of myself, I realized that all I ever did, morning or evening, was read business materials.

Even within my own peer group, my preoccupation with work was way over the line. And as I reflected on my behavior, I came to understand that much of my impatience and many of my frustrations stemmed from the unrelieved pressure of work. So I made it a point to put a little balance back into my day, at least on the way home.

But now I'm facing this challenge all over again. Not because I've relapsed, but because the new technologies of work are increasingly intrusive, tracking me down day and night and plugging me into a relentless cacophony of commerce. Just as I did once before, I've got to take the initiative myself to keep work from taking the edge off of the rest of my life. I happen to know that it's not the new technologies themselves that are the problem—because I had this problem long before these technologies exploded onto the scene. The problem is with me. I have to be the sheriff of my own life, posting notices and keeping work from trespassing where it isn't welcome. PLAY—JWS

49

THE CLEANSING POWER OF VACATIONS

Reentering the workplace after time off can be a shock to our systems. We might not be too surprised to learn that this is true after a long vacation, but researchers have found that even after a mere two-day weekend, the risk of heart attacks is greater on Monday mornings.

For years, I had no idea how to take a vacation. To leave the world of work behind and take time off is not something that comes naturally to me, and I never knew where to go to learn. I've dictated memos over a cell phone with my feet in the surf. I've excused myself from lines at theme parks to check voice mail, and I've roughed out proposals on lazy afternoons by the lake. I've even carried a fax machine cross-country to plug into a party line at a cabin in the outback. My laptop and cell phone have gone with me everywhere, tethering me to the daily affairs at work.

Reentry was never a problem for me, since I could never escape the orbit of the office to begin with. Until a few years ago, that is, when I did go off to a place where, quite without intending to, I slipped the tether of work completely. I took a commercial river trip through the Grand Canyon. Floating the Colorado River in a dory, unreachable in the depths of that wilderness, for my first time ever I was out of touch. Each day on the river arced further away from work, transporting me to an ever more tranquil state of mind, unperturbed by anything other than curiosity about the next bend in the river. On my final morning, just after breakfast, I was 'coptered out to the rim to catch a single-engine Cessna that flew me to Boulder City, and from there, I rode a bus to the Las Vegas airport for my flight home. By lunch, I was struggling with reentry. In a mere four hours, I'd left behind canyon light and shadow for a coarse neon glare that seemed to harden even the metallic clanking of the slots. Billboards blared, "Hot Sexy Shows Nightly" and "We Comp Slots" and "Buffet Morning Noon Night." People brushed past me in a furious press and rush. And as I was reaching for a phone to call the office, I froze up. Too much, too fast. I began to panic. So I retreated to a far end of the terminal where it was less noisy, and waited there in a crouch until I could board my flight.

I hadn't known to expect this. The Grand Canyon had been cathartic not only for my work life but for my ordinary life too. It had never occurred to me that life as we live it is not entirely nontoxic. Encountering life at that moment, purged of my normal habituation to it, I felt as if I'd swallowed a poison. I suddenly appreciated the cleansing power of vacations, but understood, at that same moment, the paradox of a good vacation—if reentry isn't hard, then I haven't really been away. That made me realize that for us to get a lasting benefit from time away, we must find a way to make it possible for the restorative effects of vacations to have an impact in our everyday lives. Otherwise, we lose these benefits immediately upon reentry.

The experience of the Grand Canyon has made me more conscious of the need for balance and perspective. I try to keep this sensibility close to me with a small pebble from the canyon that I carry around in my left trouser pocket. This stone is smooth and ink black, and it glistens with an even richer, deeper, speckled luster when I hold it under water, which is its natural element. When I touch this stone I am reminded of my time in the canyon. I use this memory as a chance to stop, take a breath, and be sure that at that moment I am connected to my life and my work in a balanced, fulfilling way. PLAY—JWS

50

TO PLAY, TO LIVE

Play is a function of the living, but it is not susceptible of exact definition either logically, biologically, or aesthetically.
—Johan Huizinga

When we are really playing, we know it. It's not something you can fake to yourself. When we play, we feel alive. We know that life is more than our work, however meaningful that might be. Sometimes we might try to turn our play into still another work agenda, but while golfing for business contracts, most of us are still captured by that "perfect" drive we hit. While playing catch with our young daughter to help her make the team, we laugh together. While working out to lose weight or jogging several miles to stay fit, we find our spirits soaring. Despite our best efforts at subversion, we still find ourselves at play and know that here, to be sure, is living. PLAY—RKJ

51

TURN OFF YOUR CELL PHONE

Their religion forces them to make time to connect—with one another, with their community, with God.—Edward Hallowell, M.D., describing the Sabbath practice of orthodox Jews

I spent a summer living on a moshav, or religious collective, in the Galilee region of Israel. My wife and I lived with one of the families in their home. During the week we were involved in an archeological dig. On Friday afternoons, a pot of stew would be put on the stove to simmer, door locks would be opened, and gates would be lowered at each end of the town's main street, blocking any traffic into or out of the small town for the duration of the Sabbath. After dusk, people would sit down for their dinner and their Sabbath prayers, and then would stroll up and down the main street, stopping in to talk to neighbors. During the week, these same people worked hard on their agricultural collective. But on the Sabbath, no work was done for twenty-four hours—not even shopping or talking on one's cell phone. There was something that felt right about this rhythm. We are to work; we are also to rest.

PLAY—RKJ

52

SPIRITUALITY IN THE MAINSTREAM

In nationwide polls conducted by Yankelovich, the percentage of Americans saying they believe to at least "some degree" in spiritualism rose from 12 percent in 1976 to 52 percent in 1998. Faith healing, from 10 to 45 percent; astrology, from 17 to 37 percent; reincarnation, from 9 to 25 percent; mysticism, from 2 to 15 percent; even voodoo, from 1 to 9 percent.

We're putting our money where our soul is. There's a spiritual revival sweeping across America that we see as much in how we shop as in how we pray. Network line-ups are filled with hit shows about spirituality. Magazines are packed with information and ideas about simplification and balance. Financial companies tell us more about what can't be bought than what can be. Automakers promise a Zen-like moment of peace while driving their cars. Best-seller lists are filled with spiritual how-to and self-help books—not to mention a whole host of other closely related things: Aromatherapy. Day spas. Vitamins and supplements. Gardening. Labyrinths. Alternative medicine. Stress management. Eastern mystics as corporate gurus. Business casual. Even politicians have started talking about spirituality and transcendence, which is proof positive that it's no longer a trend, it's the mainstream! Now we have an opportunity like never before to create a balance of life and work in our lives. Establishing balance no longer requires that we swim against the current. Of course, getting balance is still not as easy as a float downstream, but as a mainstream aspiration we have whatever permission we need to do whatever is needed to give it a go. SPIRITUALITY—JWS

53

REMEMBER YOUR CALLING

According to survey research cited by George Gallup, Jr., 78 percent of Americans feel the need in their lives to experience spiritual growth.

Those early monastics had something right when they vowed to spend half their days in work and the other half in prayer, contemplation, and reflection. The monastics valued all of the important things; things too important be lost in a life focused only on work. Many today are following the example of the early monastics. Books exploring traditional monastic prayers and practices have become bestsellers. Celtic spirituality is big business. Buddhist retreat centers are full. Over a million people a year go for retreats at Catholic centers. Thomas Merton might have sparked our interest in the spiritual disciplines, but writers like Kathleen Norris and Thomas Keating are extending it.

Our desire for spiritual growth can help us balance the role of work in our lives. If work is not to become a fixation, we need to develop our listening skills for the Spirit that dwells within and beyond us. Only then will we respond in gratitude to the gift of life that has been given us. Only then will our jobs become what they were meant to be—a vocation, a calling.   SPIRITUALITY—RKJ

54
SOMETHING BEYOND

It is said that even the greatest and most accomplished among us believe that there is something beyond that for which they are the undisputed masters. Great surgeons, great generals, indeed, the great masters of all professions and domains, feel that there is something beyond the limits of their skills and achievements.

It is the "something beyond" that sustains all of us through the unexpected twists and turns of life. Once I was on a flight from Atlanta to Newark that lost an engine shortly after take-off. We made an emergency landing in Greenville, South Carolina, that was the quietest landing I've ever experienced. Not only were we landing without the noise of one engine, everyone on the flight was total-ly silent. As we shared our experiences with each other later in the terminal, we all agreed that during those few moments, there was a sense of something beyond that sus-tained us and calmed us and quieted us. The sense of something beyond isn't only about great feats of medicine and war; it's mostly about things that go on in our every-day lives. It is the sense of something beyond that keeps us going in the here and now.   SPIRITUALITY—JWS

55

BODY AND SOUL

Neurologists have discovered an area in the brain that, when stimulated, produces feelings of spirituality. Even people pro-fessing no religious beliefs report these feelings when this area of their brain is stimulated.

Here's a scientific discovery to marvel over! Hard proof that each of us is born with a special power inside. We are all blessed with the inborn biological capacity for spiritu-al transcendence. It means that each of us is a bit like those superheroes of our imagination who are born with superpowers that lie hidden just beneath their street clothes. Even as we see more clearly into life's inner workings, we rediscover the mysteries of life. Science brings us closer to our spirituality not further away. As journalist and science writer Rita Carter reflected, the fact that neuroscience can plot what goes on in our brains doesn't diminish religious spirituality. In fact, it only makes sense that God would have endowed us with a specific physical capacity with which to experience him.   SPIRITUALITY—JWS

56
A LEAP OF FAITH

A national survey of pet owners found 87 percent celebrate their pet's birthday; 75 percent consider their pet to have above average intelligence; 65 percent sing or dance for their pet; 53 percent take time off from work to care for their pet; 43 percent display their pet's photo at the office.

Our tabby cat Fred relishes high places. When he was younger and sprier, he would climb onto the roof of our house and then meow loudly until we'd look up and acknowledge him. Whenever we'd sit on the porch with guests, Fred would lean down over the eaves to include himself in the gathering. Some days he'd even snuggle down in a gutter to nap. One summer afternoon my wife Joy was working in the yard near the low overhang of the back porch. Joy heard Fred above her and looked up to talk to him. As she stood there talking, Fred suddenly sprang from the roof to leap into her arms! He'd never done this before, so she was taken completely by surprise, but she managed to get her arms up in time to catch him. For a moment, she was stunned by the sheer nerve of his jump, but then she was overwhelmed by the out and out trust it showed Fred had in her.

This is why we love our pets so much—their unconditional trust and affection. They smother us with every bit of the love they have to give, and we love them in return. It's a powerful value equation, one that starts with an unconditional gift of love. It makes me wonder sometimes if we humans wouldn't all get along a little better if we did the same. Or is it just the height of naïveté to think that we can actually survive, much less prosper, if we try to live by that age-old charge: "Love one another." (John 15:17 *NRSV*)

57

THE GIFT OF GRACE

"Tout est grace," meaning grace is everything, says the young priest as he lies dying in George Bernanos' The Diary of a Country Priest.

We talk a lot as if we know what the word "grace" really means. We say we are *grateful* for someone doing us a favor. We leave waiters a *gratuity*. We *congratulate* our colleagues for their successes. We label some activity *disgraceful*. But grace remains at core a mystery. As the bumper sticker reminds us, "Grace Happens."

In both the Jewish and Christian Scriptures, the word "grace" can be found associated with the mercy and compassion of "a mother's womb." It is often linked with the "eyes" of another ("to find favor in your eyes"). And preeminently, it is linked to how God chooses to see us.

That is, grace is something we receive from another, apart from any merit we have earned or any effort we have made. Grace is a gift, always connected with the mystery of another's generosity—a gift that invites our thankful response. SPIRITUALITY—RKJ

58

MORE THAN A TEMPORARY ESCAPE

When asked in a national poll conducted by Yankelovich what word best described the decade of the nineties, "stressful" was mentioned more for the nineties than for any other decade since World War II.

Surveys conducted by Yankelovich show that to cope with stress, we are increasingly turning to passive leisure activities like reading, music, and TV, and to alcohol. We are doing this even though we say we would prefer "more time with friends" over "more time alone." But friends are too much effort for many. So too is physical activity—only 27 percent report doing something physical to relieve stress. There is nothing wrong with reading, music, or TV. But if these activities take the place of relationships and physical activity, they are at best a temporary escape. Only the whole person—body, mind, and spirit—in relation with others is able to keep life in perspective and stress under control. We need to recover a better sense of our full humanity.

WHOLENESS—RKJ

59

WIPING OFF THE GAME FACE

Henry Grunwald, the former editor-in-chief of all Time, Inc. publications who also served as the U.S. ambassador to Austria, has written about his loss of vision from AMD, or age-related macular degeneration, in his book, Twilight, which ends with this observation, "I tell myself being half-blind is not a bad metaphor for the human condition."

In my heyday of burning the candle at both ends, it was a point of pride for me to keep my nonwork life at an arm's length from my work life. Personal phone calls or errands during the workday were out of the question. I tacked up no pictures of family or vacations. I booked my travel so that I was never in transit during client business hours, even if it meant getting home very late at night. I always put on a suit and my game face to go to work. My life, such as it was, was no part of my work. So as work began to demand more and more of my time, whatever life I had got squeezed even drier.

One afternoon, as I was waiting to board a flight, I saw a mother and her two small girls searching the bustling gate area. They found her husband and their father hunkered down in a seat talking on a cell phone with folders spread around him. They rushed over to hug him. I couldn't help but overhear them saying how glad they were to catch up with him as he connected through his hometown on the way from one city to the next. They spent half an hour with him before boarding was announced. Although he seemed slightly distracted the whole time, his family was ecstatic just to be around him, no matter what he had going on at the same time. Even he seemed to pick up a spring in his step as he got onto the plane and went back to work.

I don't think anyone other than me paid much attention to them, but I was suddenly disconsolate about my own work style. I realized, for the very first time, how innocuous a little bit of family is in the bigger picture of work, if not, in fact, actually invigorating and stimulating for the caliber of what we do. Why not kiss your wife and hug your girls as you're connecting flights? Life is all around me at work these days, from small things like photos to big things like spirituality. In giving way to the priorities of my life, my work is changing character for the better. No longer does my work stand separate and apart, shouldering life aside. Now my work must accommodate my life. Work is better, and life is, too—because now work is truly a living.

WHOLENESS—JWS

60

WHY MISS A NICE DAY?

The streets are full of admirable craftsmen, but so few practical dreamers.—Man Ray

William McDonough is the dean of the University of Virginia School of Architecture and a visionary with regard to today's design. When he begins a new project, he does not first ask his potential clients what kind of building they want. Instead, he asks, "How do we love all children, all species, all time?" Such utopianism will sound impractical to most, even bizarre. But the results have won McDonough admirers worldwide.

McDonough's Coffee Creek Center in Indiana is designed in a compact way to combat sprawl and disconnection. His environmental studies center at Oberlin College is equipped to produce more energy from sunlight than it consumes. And his design for the Gap office complex in Silicon Valley includes roofs planted with wildflowers, paints with low toxicity, and fifteen-foot ceilings with windows that bring people to the sky. "When it's a nice day," says McDonough, "why feel as if you've missed it?" With typical philosophical language he says, "Design is the first signal of human intention." There is more to work than work. There is also the dream.   WHOLENESS—RKJ

61

SPACE FOR LIFE

"campus" (from Latin, campus, plain, field)

In architecture, we have worked to design distinctive buildings for our cities, but we have not worried as often about the spaces around them—the "campus." However, it is often the voids, the open spaces, that make all the difference in an architectural project, that put not only buildings but also people into conversation with each other. Think of Chicago's plazas with their public sculptures, or even the painted cows that were sprinkled throughout the city during the summer of 1999. Or think of the "campo," the plazas, in Italy. The buildings might be grand, but the fountains, the walkways, and the outdoor cafes are what make one's vacation there memorable.

Here is a metaphor regarding our lives. We too need to have space, both to frame our buildings and to exhibit our "cows" and "sculptures." Although what we build might be grand, it is often the fountains, the walkways, and the outdoor cafes that make more of a lasting impression on others. It is often the times when we are simply there for another, when we volunteer at a hospital, or when we stop over at a friend's house on the spur of the moment that matter most. Many times we have neglected the larger campus that can provide perspective and invite conversation.

WHOLENESS—RKJ

62

AFTER MIDNIGHT

John Stuart Mill observed that either tranquility or excitement could make us happy. Tranquil, we are content with less. Excited, we can put up with more pain.

I'm on a plane for business three or four days a week. Quite often, I'm asked how I can stand being on the road that much. I'm tempted to say I've just gotten used to the pain because air travel for business is irreducibly irritating. Fighting traffic, jockeying for a parking space, standing in lines, getting hassled at security, being jostled by crowds, eating bad food and paying too much for it, dealing with delays, arguing with cabbies, rushing to meetings, cramming my case into the overhead bin. No matter how smooth the flight itself, the total experience is always a hassle. When airlines send me special offers and bonuses to reward me for my above-average patronage, it only serves to irritate me yet again by reminding me how much of my life is spent on a plane.

But the truth is, this kind of business travel is not without its psychological rewards. Much of what makes it tolerable is the thrill of the chase. Closing the big sale. Making the big presentation. Leading the big assignment. Making a big impression. The fever pitch of business smoothes over the inherent indignities of business travel. These kinds of rewards can help compensate for the costs. Yet, while this keeps me going, even makes me happy, it also gets me thinking. Have I found a genuine equilibrium or just a way to distract myself from the pain? Are the rewards long-lasting or will the pain eventually break through? Am I just putting off the inevitable, a day when I will be forced to give up this adrenaline high for something less frenetic, indeed, more tranquil? And if so, why not do it now?

The ultimate answer to the question of how I'm able to keep at it is that I've learned to put my business travel in perspective and to approach my business travel in a way that keeps it from overwhelming the rest of my life. Once or twice a year, I'm on a delayed flight that doesn't get in until well after midnight. At that hour, the airport is a different place. The monitors are blank, the TVs are off, the lights are dimmed. Restaurants and shops are empty and locked. No crowds mill at the gates. The planes are all parked. The only activity is maintenance—carpets being shampooed, paint being touched up, escalators being repaired. In the middle of the night, there's none of the buzz and hum of the middle of the day. That's when I'm able to see that the electricity of travel—both the good and the bad, both the energy and the shock—is something we bring with us, not something that's already there, waiting in reserve. As I scurry to my car on these late, late nights, I can't help but reflect that both the pain and the excitement of business travel is something we impose on ourselves, so how we experience this travel is entirely within our control. Certainly, business travel is a big deal, but I no longer see it as enough of a big deal for me to get competitive or aggressive or angry about it anymore. I know now that whatever irritation I carry home from the airport is largely of my own doing and that whatever travel crisis I may have had during the business day is long forgotten by the time the maintenance crews arrive.

WHOLENESS—JWS

63

SEEKING THE STILLNESS

Sometimes, in a summer morning, having taken my accustomed bath, I sat in my sunny doorway from sunrise till noon, rapt in reverie.—Henry David Thoreau

Thoreau wanted breathing room, both figuratively and literally, so much so that he moved to Walden Pond. There, removed from the city and from the obligations of everyday life, he was often content to do nothing but sit. After a time of protracted idleness, he would return to his work, refreshed and renewed. For most of us, such a lifestyle seems as distant as Walden Pond. Our calendars are so full that we even have to write in the margins to remember everything we've scheduled. But at some deep level we also know that it is in the spaces in life that our spirits are nourished.

When I was a college dean, I would say to the faculty: "During your semester sabbatical leave, you can do two of the following three things. You can stay at home and work at keeping your regular commitments going. You can complete a major writing or research project. Or you can refresh and renew yourself. But you can't accomplish all three." I knew this from personal experience. Somehow we, unlike Thoreau, have a hard time accepting that being still and doing "nothing" can refresh and renew in such a complete way that our whole life—work, family relationships, community involvement—is revitalized. Though most of us don't have the option of an extended sabbatical, we need to use the spaces we have—a few moments of stillness after we get up in the morning, a quiet lunch in the park, or a long weekend away from home. Seeking the stillness, as Thoreau did, is a first step in finding refreshment for our spirits.

WHOLENESS—RKJ

64
DOING ONE THING

A newspaper story about multitasking told of one mother who recalled the day she told her six-year-old daughter not to waste time by just sitting on the potty, but to brush her teeth and her hair at the same time. The mother said to the reporter that as soon as she said this, she caught herself, realizing at that moment that her multitasking had gotten out of control.

Nowadays dead time is not having nothing to do; it's having only one thing to do. Like showering. Or sleeping. Or driving to work. Or going to the symphony or the ballet. Or reading *War and Peace*. Or even being a six-year-old sitting on the potty. We keep trying to devise ways to turn each of these activities into multitasking opportunities. What are we making room for? More multitasking? What is the last refuge from multitasking?

Is there any single activity left that we can do guilt free? I asked around. One friend said meditation. Another friend said confession. Yet another said solitary confinement. One morbid friend said it's when we are dying, and one smart-aleck friend assured me it's sex. As for me, I'm not sure we're safe until we find some alternatives that we prefer to multitasking—something that seems worth our undivided attention. Multitasking just happens to strike us as the superior way to spend our time. Our challenge is not escaping multitasking so much as it is rediscovering what's worth our single-minded attention. Before we can feel good about stopping and smelling the roses, we have to feel bad that we aren't, that simply "being busy" is a poor excuse for missing out on the simple beauty of life.

EMPOWERMENT—JWS

65
AN END TO FORGETTING

Even the best jugglers know that if you do it non-stop long enough, sooner or later, a ball will fall.

There was a year not too long ago when I simply couldn't keep up with anything. In twelve months, I lost two cell phones, an organizer, a calculator, my calendar, a felt hat, a sport coat, two pairs of gloves, a portable CD player, a fancy pen, a pair of sunglasses, an alarm clock, even a laptop. Nothing was stolen. I would just set something down on a business trip, forget about it, and then leave it behind. It created constant inconvenience because that year was also the single busiest year I've had so far in my career. I was leading two multimillion dollar, yearlong projects, splitting my time between two clients on opposite coasts. Nights and weekends were devoted to catching up on everything else at work. I had little time to spare.

I stayed on top of all the work, though, and saw that it was completed successfully. But the frustration of constantly losing things was driving me to distraction. I just couldn't understand how someone as obsessive and as controlling as myself could be so careless and forgetful. The harder I tried to keep up, the more I seemed to lose. I was whining about this one afternoon to one of my clients. She listened sympathetically, but then told me there was no mystery here. The problem was simple: I was just too busy. My mind was overfull from overwork, so anything peripheral to my main concerns and priorities was quickly dropped and forgotten. No matter how much I tried, I simply couldn't be anything other than distracted and scat-terbrained about things not directly related to work. And having made that diagnosis, she then demanded, as the client, that I get more help on her project. I did, and to my amazement her assessment turned out to be exactly right. In no time at all, I lost my absentmindedness.

Just as she had pointed out to me, my ability to man-age my life had as much to do with how much I was doing as it did with how I was doing it. To leave some time unclaimed so that the rest of my time can be properly managed and contained is a lesson I've not forgotten, and it's something I now make a point of remembering as I schedule my time and plan ahead.   EMPOWERMENT—JWS

66
ROMANTICIZING THE PAST

Oh, for the good ol' days.

Most of us long for the serenity of the seventies when we had time for our families, for barbecues on the patio, and for evenings at home. I lived in the late seventies with my young family in a mid-sized town in Kentucky. Life was certainly less frantic than our current lifestyle in Southern California. Rather than fifty cultural events to choose from, there were two each weekend. Rather than exorbitant prices, life was affordable.

But we can easily romanticize our past. Juggling schedules and multitasking are not recently acquired skills. Overcommitment and the drivenness that accompanies it predate the seventies. And the cause has more to do with our inner needs than with changing outer circumstances. As we seek to deal with the drivenness of our lives today, we need to rediscover one of the most important words in our vocabulary, "No." If we do, we will again be able to say "Yes" to those times with our families, those barbecues on the patio, and those evenings at home.

EMPOWERMENT—RKJ

67

TIME BETTER SPENT

According to the Bureau of Labor Statistics, the average work week has increased by almost two hours since 1982. At the same time, the percentage of married couples who both work has increased over the same period from 39 percent to 47 percent, further intensifying time pressures on families.

The only way we can stay even moneywise is to fall behind timewise. But there may be a way to turn this time squeeze into a good thing. In my own struggle with it, I've taken a long look at what I do away from work and questioned the importance of each and every thing. With no choice but to prioritize, I decided to make sure that I was spending my free time only on the essentials without over-scheduling the free time available to me. Some of what I've kept in my free time is structured time to get projects done or activities completed. But the largest portion of my free time is unstructured time in which my family and I are free to invent the moment, so to speak. Nothing is pressuring us. No deadlines are hanging over us. We turn to each other, not to the to-do list, to figure out what's next. As a result, I feel far better about my free time than ever before. Because even as my free time is being squeezed by work, I am much more certain that I am keeping misspent free time to a minimum.   EMPOWERMENT—JWS

68
SEARCHING FOR SIMPLICITY

Nationwide surveys conducted by Yankelovich show that 76 percent of Americans are looking for ways to simplify their lives. And over half feel a strong need to shed non-essential things from their lives.

Magazines show us easier ways to grill, five-minute make-up strategies, tips for packing light, ways to keep the table simple, and fabrics that require less care. We can pay our bills online, relegate useless knickknacks to the yard sale, and reorganize our lives. We can go from the mailbox to the recycling bin and sort our mail there. We can listen to books on tape while we drive. We can set a schedule on Sundays for the week. There is even a Web site to share ideas with each other about how to simplify our lives. All of these suggestions have merit. But we know they are not the solution.

Most of us are eating breakfast more quickly, if at all. We spend less time volunteering at church or in the community. And we wish we knew more people as good friends. Recreational activities have been lessening for several years now. And our stress count is going up. We suspect that some essentials are being left out, yet we find it difficult to change.

It is not enough to multitask, to be more efficient, or to eliminate the extras. We just find more tasks and chores to fill the vacant moments. What's more important is to identify two or three priorities that would add rhythm and meaning to our lives. Maybe we still want to coach our kid's soccer team. Or we wish that the after-dinner walk with our spouse at sunset while the kids do the dishes could be sacrosanct. It is a commitment to better balance, not just a more efficient use of time, that will bring satisfaction.   EMPOWERMENT—RKJ

69

BONUS YEARS

Life expectancy during the early Christian era in Rome was 22.0 years. During the early Colonial era in the U.S., it was only 35.5; by 1900, it was 49.2. Today, life expectancy in the U.S. is 76.1.

One hundred years ago, the average person in America lived to be forty-nine years old. Now it is seventy-six. A bonus of almost thirty years! How are we to understand this gift of life? When young, play is central, as we explore the variety and wonder of the world around us. In adulthood, work predominates as we discover our gifts and interests and seek to live out our vocation. Can our mature years not be characterized by a better balance of both work and play? Even after our retirement we need not cease working nor should we give up playfully exploring life's fullness. Instead, we have an extra three decades to embrace both.

Volunteering. Helping children. Working part-time. Taking courses. Writing. The list of work-related activities outside or beyond our regular professions is as broad as life itself. But so too for our play. Off-season travel to Europe now surpasses travel in the summer months due to the booming numbers of seniors and those without children at home. Having time for friends and family can increase as children move out of the house. An appreciation of a variety of cultural activities can deepen, building on tastes that have developed earlier in life.

Play. Work. Work and play. The synthesis invites our thanksgiving.   EMPOWERMENT—RKJ

70

LIFE IS TOO IMPORTANT

I never want to forget the raw fear of cancer or the prospect of death.—Hamilton Jordan

Hamilton Jordan, when he worked for President Carter, was the youngest chief of staff in history. Seemingly, he could do anything he wanted. But Hodgkin's lymphoma at age forty, skin cancer at forty-six, and prostate cancer at age fifty have given him a new outlook toward life. True, he worked at beating cancer with the same energy and single-mindedness that he brought to politics. But now life seems different. Jordan has new priorities. He finds time to fix breakfast for his kids and take them to school. Political ambition no longer consumes; resentment no longer rules. Why? Because life is too important.

STRENGTH—RKJ

71
LOOKING A HERO IN THE FACE

Suffering produces endurance, and endurance produces character, and character produces hope.
—St. Paul (Romans 5:3–4 NRSV)

I was with a friend recently whose wife suffers excruciating pain because the dead cells that her body should slough off are somehow wrongly stored in her bones replacing her marrow. All this because she lacks one enzyme. Life is, at best, a chore for this couple. Yet, they have a deep love, even a reverence, for the gift of life with which they have been blessed.

The ethicist Stanley Hauerwas has written, "Heroism is not to be identified with those that can 'do something,' but rather is to be found in those who persevere through suffering. . . . Our healing is not the overcoming of our illnesses, but rather our ability to share our going on with one another through the community our stories create." If this is true, and I think it is, my friends are heroes. Just like some of the classic texts in spirituality, they have looked suffering in the face and have penetrated behind its mystery to the fragile joy of life. A stripping away of life's trappings has brought more, not less.   STRENGTH—RKJ

72

THE GIFT OF DISCIPLINE

Don't be afraid of the dark. Remember, we need the night to see the stars.—Joey Reiman

Let's not kid ourselves. When bad things happen, they're still bad things no matter what good may come from them. Yet, at the same time, if something good does come out of something bad, we shouldn't let it go unrecognized or unappreciated. We may even find something redeeming there. Is this not the lesson of the cross?

I've had diabetes my entire adult life. It's a daily concern, a constant constraint on how I live and the risks I take. The medical complications of poor control are not insignificant, so I take it seriously. I manage my lifestyle to keep my diabetes under control. This is the good that has come from something bad. Diabetes has given me a gift, the gift of discipline.

My diabetes has actually made me healthier because to control it—something I have come to take very seriously in recent years—I must be moderate and smarter in all that I do and eat. Of course, I can do and eat anything; I just can't take anything for granted. I must exercise. I must eat less. I must eat better. I must manage stress. I must go to the doctor regularly. I am regularly tempted to break my discipline, and on occasion I do. But my diabetes is always there to get me back on track. Without it, I'm not sure I would be able to sustain this discipline. This is my advantage relative to many other people. So, all in all, I am spared from the worst elements of our increasingly sedentary, overindulgent, high-risk lifestyles because I have a chronic disease. My diabetes is something that, as incredible as this seems even to me, I would be scared to lose as a source of strength and focus in my life. STRENGTH—JWS

73

DANCING OVER DECORUM

David danced before the Lord with all his might; David was girded with a linen ephod. So David and all the house of Israel brought up the ark of the Lord with shouting, and with the sound of the trumpet. As the ark of the Lord came into the city of David, Michal, daughter of Saul, looked out of the window, and saw King David leaping and dancing before the Lord; and she despised him in her heart.—2 Samuel 6: 14–16 (NRSV)

When Israel's King David recovered the ark of the Lord and brought it again to Jerusalem, he was so filled with joy that he stripped to his underwear and began dancing with his people. Here was an occasion for partying if there ever were such an occasion. But Michal, David's wife, became angry with him for failing to behave like a king, for not acting regally. Matters of propriety and station were every-thing to her. In this biblical story of a family dispute, God takes the side of David. For God, dancing in joy is more important than working at one's decorum.   JOY—RKJ

74

A TIME TO LAUGH

For everything there is a season ... a time to plant, and a time to pluck up what is planted ... a time to weep, and a time to laugh ... a time for war, and a time for peace.—Ecclesiastes 3:1–8 (NRSV)

In 1862 as the Civil War raged, Abraham Lincoln called his inner circle of advisers together for a cabinet meeting, only to read them words from the humorist Artemus Ward. As Lincoln laughed heartily, his colleagues sat silently disapproving. The President chided them for not laughing. Lincoln went on to explain to his coworkers that given the strain he was continually under, if he did not laugh he thought he might actually die. Lincoln then turned to the work at hand, discussing with his associates a draft of a paper he had just written. It was the Emancipation Proclamation, which abolished slavery in the Confederate States. There is a time to laugh and a time to weep! A time for war and a time for peace!   JOY—RKJ

75

MADE BY HAND

Naturalist and author Craig Childs has written of a day he spent in the deep forest of an island off the coast of British Columbia watching six bald eagles in their aeries atop the Sitka spruce. Later at camp near dinnertime, one of these eagles soared over- head and Craig saw a feather fall from its wing. Suddenly, in Craig's words, "I am running as if the sky had just caught fire and I am trying to catch the very first ember." Craig described his emotions during the moment after as he looked in his hands at the feather he had just collected: "I unfold my fingers and look into the hollow formed there as if I have taken hold of a piece of flight and wildness itself."

My wife, Joy, collects Christmas tree ornaments. Since high school, she's been browsing stores and antique shops and catalogs and sale tables for unusual and distinctive things to hang on our tree. Every year she takes a few days out of her schedule to bring her boxes up from the basement, unpack them, organize the ornaments and lights, and then decorate the tree. The end result is spectacular.

Every ornament tells a story. Every ornament has a connection to some shared memory or to some bit of adventure or elation in our lives together. There's one with a date from every year of our marriage. There are several with the logos and mascots of our college alma mater. There are characters from the Christmas stories and children's movies of our childhood. There are pairs of every kind of creature from a handmade Noah's ark collection. There are balls made by Native American artists and Southern craftsmen. There are personalized ornaments for all of our old house addresses, and even a few with the name of our cat. Joy's ornaments are made from all types of materials—some glass, some clay, some wooden, some silver, a few are crystal. She has limited edition strings of lights as well as complete sets of collectibles that were offered only a few at a time over several-year periods.

She's bought ornaments in every place we've lived or visited, from New England to the Southwest, from London to Hawaii. I like to share in her tree-decorating ritual by watching her concentrate on getting every item in just the right place. This, to me, is a handmade Christmas—not because she made the ornaments, but because of the way these ornaments are organized and hung and shared with our family. My wife carries this spirit with her year round as she hunts for more to collect, for more to brighten the tree she decorates for our enjoyment at Christmastime. This is her handmade gift to us, and one that we look forward to every year.

JOY—JWS

76

LINGERING WITH GOOD FRIENDS

I eat breakfast in my car. Eating cereal requires a lot of talent.
I do it at stoplights.—Stephanie Crouse, a commuter
from El Paso, Texas

Too often we eat on the run. We fail to let mealtimes be a source of renewal. The rush of breakfast is often worst, but other meals suffer from the lack of time we give to them as well. Often when eating out, we are not even allowed to slow down. Waiters remove plates while our companions are still eating. It is impossible to linger over our last bites of pasta or to savor that chocolate torte. A friend of mine who is a restaurant manager in Seattle switches to ever more edgy music as his eatery fills up, knowing he can subconsciously get his guests to hurry their meals so they'll leave and make room for others.

But go to a restaurant in Italy. When you reserve a table for dinner, you often have the table for the evening. If you seem to be in a hurry, the waiter might even ply you with more pasta or an extra glass of wine. The server expects you to linger with good friends over a dark brew. After all, a cup of coffee is not pleasurable unless there's time to enjoy it. No attempt to have two or three sittings here. The Italians know a meal should not be gobbled nor should it be one of several tasks going on simultaneously. It should be savored. It should be a pause—a parenthesis in life that refreshes both body and spirit.   JOY—RKJ

77

PURPOSEFUL PLAY

Play oxygenates life, giving it a freshness and vitality that work alone misses.

When we come right down to it, many of us are not good players. Yes, we might be good team players or corporate players, but we are lousy "play" players. Play seems to have no point. By definition, it is to have no reason beyond itself; it is "purposeless" activity. Thus, we think play suitable only for children. Even our dictionaries leave us with the wrong impression, describing "play" as the "impulsive activity of children."

But play is not something we should grow out of. There is a purposefulness to its purposelessness. Play has no reason beyond itself, and yet the results of our play are far-reaching: a sense of joy and delight, an affirmation of our whole self, the creation of a bond with the world, the emancipation of our spirits, the revitalization of our workaday world. Play might be nonutilitarian, but it is nonetheless productive.

JOY—RKJ

78

FREE TO PLAY

Researchers have noted a decline in the amount of time children spend each day in free play—about 30 minutes less since 1981. As parents find their schedules more frantic and time-pressured, they turn to organized activities as a means of providing care and supervision for their kids. All of which makes childhood more stressful than ever before.

What is it that troubles us about these statistics? Is it a legitimate concern that today's teens are facing ever greater stress and demands on their time? After all, such demands on teens are nothing new. Throughout history, teens have had to step into highly stressful situations and roles on the stage of world events. At fourteen, Richard II put down a rebellion, Rossini conducted an orchestra, Alexander Hamilton drew up trading rules for the firm that employed him, and Catherine de Médicis was married to the fourteen year-old duc de Orléans, who later became Henry II of France. So is it unreasonable for us to want more for our children than days spent lolling around with nothing productive to do? We want our children to be accomplished, especially because we see that their best opportunities are so much more competitive than they used to be. Maybe what troubles us is not the loss of free play but that the bar of success has been set so much higher that every element of childhood, even free play, has become a competition.

A friend of mine was talking one day about how his eleven-year-old son was unwilling to spend time doing anything at which he had no shot at being the very best. His son had tried and given up on baseball, basketball, soccer, skating, archery, piano, guitar, trombone, and art. All his son did now was play electronic games online, which was the one thing at which his son could be assured of winning. My friend said his son lacked no dedication, commitment, or work ethic. Rather, the pressure to be on top had corrupted his son's capacity to simply enjoy himself at something irrespective of his relative skills and abilities. My friend worried that this was narrowing his son's horizons and undermining his son's ability to appreciate true excellence. My friend lamented that some stigma his son felt about being second best was keeping his son from the very best kind of well-rounded life. In particular, my friend fretted that perhaps he himself had had a hand in conveying this competitive imperative to his son by organizing his son's schedule like his own in which every moment of every day is filled with a succession of activities, projects, and goals.

Like my friend and many other baby boomers, I remember my childhood years as different from today. I grew up with lots of free time to kill, climbing trees, riding bikes, splashing through creeks, and playing kick-the-can with the neighborhood gang late into a summer's day until our mothers called us home in the gathering dusk. Free play was a sort of youthful accomplishment back then—a chance to escape and explore that we took for granted. But more is required today. Indeed, I look back on my grades and test scores and realize that had I applied to my college alma mater today I wouldn't even have been wait-listed, much less accepted!

The pressure is greater nowadays, so balance can no longer be presumed, and our lifestyles are not always good role models for our kids. Balance is not something our kids are likely to learn and pick up on their own because balance is not something they encounter much anymore. So we must make a point of teaching balance to our kids, which starts, perhaps, with a better example from us.

STRESS—JWS

79

CHRONIC STRESS

Medical authorities believe that many of the ailments treated by family doctors today are stress-related—headaches, ulcers, irritable bowel, fatigue, chronic pain syndrome, insomnia, and others.

One Protestant denomination that provides its own health plan for its clergy and religious workers tracked what medicines were being prescribed to pastors and their families. The most commonly used drug was Prozac. The next two most commonly used medicines were for headaches and the next two were for ulcers. This suggests that even for church leaders, those men and women who try to be role models, the five most commonly prescribed drugs were related to stress-induced illnesses. You might wish that faith did something to improve our health, but in the case of stress, society drowns it out. Perhaps these clergy have over-personalized the hymn, *Work for the Night Is Coming*. Instead, they need to sing daily, *He's Got the Whole World in His Hands.*

STRESS—RKJ

80

PUBLIC HEALTH ENEMY NUMBER ONE

Constant unrelieved stress endangers our health and well-being. Our immune system is weakened, biological and genetic processes are interrupted and distorted, brain cells die, and our systems overflow with an unnatural flood of hormones and bodily chemicals.

An uncle of mine once told me that the art of horse trading was all about paying the seller no more than half the value you saw in something. Why? Because, he said, no matter what you pay, you always wind up spending that much again to keep whatever you've bought in good enough repair to get what you want out of it. If we hold to my uncle's concept of a bargain, we may begin to realize that how we live nowadays is just not worth it.

Clearly, the human race wasn't made to run a marathon rat race, which is why stress is now the biggest threat to public health. To sustain our pace, we pay too great a price in stress, indeed, far more than we can afford to pay to put ourselves back into good repair. That's no bargain. Finding ways to manage stress has become as important to the future of our public health as public sanitation and vaccinations were in the past. We need to do some smarter "horse trading" to make sure we don't pay too high a price for the ways we live our lives.

This need not be a wholesale turnover in what we do. A lot of times it's just a matter of renegotiating how we do things. I used to travel for business by a rule I called six-and-six, which meant irrespective of when my meetings were scheduled I would travel out on the 6 A.M. flight and travel back no earlier than a 6 P.M. flight. That way, I was never in the air during business hours. Since I was on the road three or four days a week, traveling by the rule of six-

and-six meant that I was rarely at home and that I never got more than a few hours of sleep. This took a toll. I ate poorly and exercised little. I gained weight. I became irascible and sullen and forgetful. I lost any sense of connection or constancy in my life. Early one morning on my drive to the airport, the pain of what I was doing to myself finally became unbearable and I screamed out at the top of my lungs how much I hated how I was living. I pounded the steering wheel in frustration and swerved off the interstate to stop and swear at myself for making such a poor bargain with my life. From that moment forward, I dropped the rule of six-and-six. Nowadays, I keep up by working smarter. Indeed, I found that the six-and-six rule didn't matter much in my success. Today, I get just as much done as ever before, but the price I pay at work no longer costs me my life.   STRESS—JWS

81

RELATIVE WEALTH

A 1995 nationwide survey commissioned by the Merck Family Fund found that over one-quarter of those in households with incomes of $100,000 or more don't feel they have enough to buy all they need; indeed, one in five said they spent every penny they earned on the basic necessities.

It isn't only what we make that matters but also what we spend. We all know people who thrive on little and others that rack up huge credit card debts while having hefty salaries. A professor and his wife that we know had four children and took in more foster kids. Yet they always had plenty of money despite their low single salary (less than $20,000 in the late 1970s). He was a farm boy from Iowa who enjoyed planting a garden and fixing a roof as much as he enjoyed Kant and Augustine. If consumption is moderated, then balance in one's work and nonwork priorities has a fighting chance.

MATERIALISM—RKJ

82

PRIORITIES NOT PRUDENCE

A 1997 survey asked the wealthiest one percent of Americans (those with a net worth of at least $2.5 million) how much they would pay for various sources of happiness, such as the following:

A place in heaven ....$640,000 on average

True love ....$487,000 on average

Great intellect ....$407,000 on average

Being president ....$55,000 on average

Most of us can understand the $55,000, given both the stress and the spotlight of the presidency. But why just $640,000 to ensure a place in heaven? Indeed, what becomes of the remaining $1,860,000?

Jesus once told a story about a rich farmer who was wildly successful. Having no place to store his goods and his grain, he decided to tear down his barns and build larger ones. His goal, he said, was to provide more amply for his retirement, so he would be able to "relax, eat, drink, be merry." But in Jesus' parable, God responded to the farmer's desire for ever more possessions by saying,

"'You fool! This very night your life is being demanded of you. And the things you have prepared, whose will they be?'" (Luke 12:20 *NRSV*)

Jesus' story is not about having money but about the hoarding that often accompanies this. It is not about prudence but priorities. Jesus goes on to tell his listeners that they should not worry about what they will eat or what they will wear, for like the birds, God will provide for them. If we focus our attention and resources on what is of most value to us, then the rest will be provided.

MATERIALISM—RKJ

83
A RICHER CURRENCY OF LIFE

In a 2000 nationwide poll of kids 9 to 14 years of age commissioned by Nickelodeon/Time, 23 percent said they would rather be rich and unhappy than poor and happy, up from 14 percent saying so a year earlier.

The apple falls close to the tree. Golden apples, it seems. Our kids want the good life as much as we do, and we should be happy that they're so ambitious. But will they be happy in the end? Indeed, what have they learned from us about wealth and contentment? Have we, by our example, taught a growing number of kids that it's better to be rich than happy? Are we letting slip small hints that deep down we believe riches and happiness are like different blood types that can't course through the same veins? Do our kids sense that we believe we have wound up living a lot better but feeling a lot worse than we ever expected?

It would be wrong, of course, to paint a frown on the face of every rich guy we see. Perhaps it's our language that's a bit fuzzy here. I suspect it's not happiness that's the issue so much as it is fulfillment, which is exactly what we parents and adults are struggling with ourselves nowadays. It should be no surprise then that more and more of our kids seem to be concluding that fulfillment is elusive and, perhaps, beside the point, so grab the money, and lots of it, while you can. Riches are sort of like plan B: if you can't get fulfillment—call it happiness—at least you've got the cash. Jesus cautioned us: "How hard it is for those who have wealth to enter the kingdom of God!

Indeed, it is easier for a camel to go through the eye of a needle than for someone who is rich to enter the kingdom of God." (Luke 18:24–25 *NRSV*) This isn't because money is bad or sinful per se, but because a fixation on money often chokes off concern or energy for anything else. Like being happy or fulfilled. Like caring for others, or even for our own souls.

If our predicament is that we can't live better because we're too well off, then money is indeed a problem. The solution for this is not poverty but new priorities. Our kids should see that being rich and unhappy is not simply an option to choose or not to choose. The fact that a growing number of kids are willing to accept unhappiness in exchange for wealth is a danger signal that our value equation is not balanced and that what we require instead of riches is a richer currency of life. MATERIALISM—JWS

84
LOTS OF LESS

Even in the midst of the enormous prosperity of the nineties, Americans felt more at sea than ever before. Disconnected from family, from core values, from God, people were searching for more even as they were pocketing more. This discontent remains with us like a pot aboil, ready to explode.

Money talks, but what is it saying to us? Prosperity gives us more and more, but in lots of ways we still don't have what we really need. There are some big issues here about spirituality, charity, and inequality that have become part of our national agenda. But we're most likely to encounter this gap between prosperity and satisfaction in more mundane ways. A friend of mine and his wife were headed to a wedding one Saturday afternoon. They left a few minutes early so that they could run an errand on the way. They stopped at a bath supply superstore to buy a plastic soap dish for their guest bathroom. Expecting to grab something and go, they ran into the store and turned the corner to the soap-dish aisle. My friend said later, "All we wanted was an inexpensive soap dish with some nonde-script pattern. I figured this would be simple. How could you make a mistake buying a cheap plastic soap dish? But when we got to that section of the store, there were about seventy-five choices stacked up in front of us, and I froze. I suddenly realized there were seventy-four different ways to be wrong!" Stymied by too many options and short on time, my friend and his wife ran back out without buying anything at all.

Too many choices can add up to one big bad thing. Too much of something can be stressful too. And these days, inundated with stuff to buy, we're searching harder than ever for the true stuff of life. MATERIALISM—JWS

85
THE WHOLE PERSON

It was the best of times, it was the worst of times, it was the age of wisdom, it was the age of foolishness.—Charles Dickens

David Myers begins his book *The American Paradox: Spiritual Hunger in an Age of Plenty* with Dickens's reflection. Since 1960, the average American has doubled real income, eats out two and a half times more often, and pays less for air travel and hamburgers. Yet the average middle-income couple with children works an average of eight weeks more than in 1979 and spends twenty-two fewer hours a week with their children than in 1969. Our divorce rate has doubled, our prison population has quintupled, and the number of babies born to unmarried parents has increased seven times. Ours wallets might be fatter, but our souls are leaner.

Prosperity has had its price. Few question this conclusion. What to do? Some cope by opting off the treadmill. Simplifying is surely part of the answer, but the nurture of a balanced life seems even more central. Do you have supportive communities? Is your family a priority? Do you take time to become busy with things you truly feel enthusiastic about? Are you involved in helping others? Where are you learning new things? Are you opening yourself to spiritual grace? What about exercise? The list might seem daunting at first, but it is also straightforward. When it comes to happiness in life, there are few surprises. It is feeding the whole person that will collectively meet our spiritual hunger. Bon appétit!   MATERIALISM—RKJ

86
I SHOP THEREFORE I AM

For many of us, what we are has become closely tied to what we buy. Too often, we shop to soothe our stress and our worries and our anxieties. Aristotle counseled that our preferences come from our character. But in today's consumer-obsessed society, building character takes a back seat to deciding what to buy. Rather than deal with our insecurities we smother them beneath a mound of stuff.

My weakness is CDs. I buy a lot, indeed, far more than I can really listen to and fully appreciate. I ran out of storage room years ago, so now they pile up. There are many I've bought that I've never even played. I buy them for a number of reasons. Needless to say, I do enjoy them. Also, I fancy myself as a collector of obscure artists. And I like the fact that I can sort through them and always discover something fresh, either new or forgotten. There are other, deeper reasons too. I crave the thrill of hearing a really fabulous song for the very first time, so I'm always hoping to recreate that experience with the next CD I buy. After tough days at the office, I'll often browse a CD store as a salve for my ego. Plus, buying lots and lots of CDs is a way for me to get a leg up on music trends in order to show myself off as a person who's regarded as in the know about something.

My weakness for buying CDs may strike you as a very minor peccadillo, but it gives me pause. It reminds me that it's in the small ways as much as in the big ways that our character can show signs of material corrosion. For most of us, it doesn't take much to stay away from the big mistakes. The consequences are severe enough. What plagues us instead is the sort of challenge that tests me—everyday temptations with a big attraction that drown us a drop at a time in a pool overflowing with material abundance. MATERIALISM—JWS

87

THE OBLIGATIONS OF OWNERSHIP

In a nationwide survey commissioned by the Wall Street Journal and NBC News, three-quarters of those earning $100,000 or more a year said they have a bigger problem managing their time than managing their money. In contrast, among the population at large, money not time is more worrisome.

It's kind of hard to cut the guy driving the luxury car a break when he whines about not having enough time to enjoy himself. Those are problems to have, right? Still, it's telling that those who have more than most of us feel a little worse than the rest of us, at least when it comes to time. It's a reminder that ownership comes with obligations. The more we have, the more time we have to spend caring for it and planning around it and paying for it. As we fill our lives with stuff, we clutter our time with obligations. Cars must be tuned and polished and insured. Furniture must be dusted and shined and repaired. Art must be hung and protected and restored. Collectibles must be hunted and sorted and preserved. Music and videos must be stored and cleaned and played. Clothing must be tried on and bought and replaced. Houses must be furnished and kept up and lived in. Nothing we can have can be ours without giving us something else to do, even if only the effort it takes to afford it. The more we have, the more we have to do. It is no surprise then that those with the least time are those with the most stuff. This is not an indictment of nice things. We all want to ride in a luxury car. It's simply a reminder that whatever we aspire to own should be something we are prepared to give up the time to have. MATERIALISM-JWS

88

A NEW HOPE

Notwithstanding our unprecedented contemporary material prosperity, there is a widespread sense we all share to some degree that in many ways things were better in decades past.

We baby boomers grew up with grand expectations about the future. Swept up in the can-do, man-on-the-moon optimism of our parents' generation, we came of age believing the future would be some version of the 1964 World's Fair. We believed that we'd live in sleek, stream-lined cities and get around by monorail or hovercraft; that we'd dress in form-fitting jumpsuits made of technology-friendly, bio-enhancing materials; that robots would do our chores while we worked a mere twenty-hour work week; that we'd vanquish our social problems so that our most pressing worry would be what to do with all of our new leisure time. It was a hopeful view of the future, and it inspired us. Not that there weren't problems, but we felt we'd fix them once and for all along the way.

Unfortunately, the future didn't turn into the 1964 World's Fair; it turned into the eighties—a decade that ended in a crash, with epidemics of crime and crack and corruption, abruptly dashing our youthful expectations, and from which we're still recovering. Notwithstanding the booming nineties, we've yet to recoup the hope and trust we'd lost by the end of the eighties. So even in the wake of good times, we have remained suspicious and skeptical. Irony is our one shared sensibility. It's as if we're afraid to enjoy ourselves too much, for we've been burned in that way once before. Consequently, we're not passing onto our children the kind of high hopes for tomorrow that our parents passed onto us.

We don't have the same blind faith in the march of progress. We're certain the future will be a marvelous spectacle, but we're not at all sure we'll feel very spectacular about it when it arrives. The result is a conspicuous breach between our material wealth and our spiritual health. Ensconced in great comfort, we feel uncomfortable. But this gap is not all bad. This gap forces us to find new anchors for our faith and this gap impels us to nurture an inner peace apart from our prosperity.

Not that there's anything missing from our materialism. The rift between what we have and what we feel stems from the fact that tangibles always come up short when measured against intangible satisfactions. The problem is that we've expected too much from our mountain of stuff. So it should come at no surprise that it's let us down. We can't critique materialism for failing to deliver something that by definition it can't provide. This is our responsibility, and one we have begun to shoulder. It is a challenge to be celebrated, not lamented, for if we can rebuild a sense of spirituality to go with our materialism, we will leave behind a unique legacy—continued material progress grounded by a more powerful, more satisfying, more enriched sense of what matters and what, in the end, makes it all worthwhile. MATERIALISM—JWS

89
LOSING TO WIN

More and more, on campus and on the street, I see young people wearing T-shirts with a single word on them, Loser.

Once a term of derision or pity, "loser" is now often used as an ironic and irreverent joke by disenchanted GenXers. Rather than bemoan society's rejection, some in popular culture, whether musicians or filmmakers, are mocking it. They have opted off their parents' treadmill. They have rejected the big studios for the independents. They could care less about being part of the in crowd. They might be judged of less worth or significance, but, they seem to say, so what? The recent movie *Loser* directed by Amy

Heckerling plays with the term in this way. So too does rapper DMX who labels himself "Born Loser."

There is a certain irony in "losers" that is now becoming popular. But there is also a clear message to those of us who are judged "winners." Our success has too often come with a price—divorce, debt, stress. If this is winning, then losing has something to teach us too. Or maybe, life is not so much about competing as it is about living.

MATERIALISM—RKJ

90
TWO CLASSES

A 1995 nationwide survey commissioned by the Merck Family Fund revealed that 95 percent of Americans believe we are too materialistic and that 82 percent believe we consume more than we need. In fact, 28 percent of Americans report having voluntarily taken a pay cut in order to have a job that gives them more time and more balance in their lives.

There are two leisure classes in America. One has lots of money and the other has enough money. Millions feel they have enough, even if their net worth is far short of millions. They are sufficiently at ease with their finances to kick back some. Not that money doesn't matter, only that for many people, the threshold above which money ceases to be the thing that matters most isn't that high. So, even in the midst of our recent boom times, voluntary simplicity—the deliberate choice to make do and have more of a life with less—became a mantra for millions. Nearly one third of us have done it, and without doubt, many more of us secretly wish we could. This is a remarkably large number, and surely one of the puzzles of our contemporary collective prosperity. In the midst of so much, there is a widespread willingness to live with less.

Years back, a friend of mine was running a small ad agency he'd started when the chance arose for him throw his lot in with a bigger agency. It would have been much more work, but it would have paid him a whole lot more money. He turned it down. Of course, he had a special reason. He's diabetic, and he felt that the extra stress would have been unhealthy. More money just wasn't worth it. Not that he had lots of money, but he had enough. And what he had made it possible for him to consider other priorities as more important than money. Although his situation was unusual, his reasoning was not. It is a common line of thinking nowadays. Time spent accumulating more than enough is not necessarily time well spent, and many people have decided that in getting by with a bit less, they can get a lot more out of life.

MATERIALISM—JWS

91
THE NEW AMERICAN DREAM

In a national survey commissioned by AARP, one-third said they had no desire to be wealthy, three-quarters thought wealth would make them insensitive, and four out of five feared wealth would make them greedy.

The American dream has always been about making it, and about making as much of it as possible. What, then, do we make of so many Americans disavowing any interest in being wealthy? It's not sour grapes. Only a very small percentage of the respondents in that survey said they felt left out of the economic boom of the nineties. Instead, there seems to be a sentiment afoot that just as clothes make the man, so too do riches make one's character, and more and more of us see wealth as unbecoming.

The economic boom made it impossible for us to ignore how unsatisfied we are. In the past, we could blame our discontent on the economy. No longer. And not only do we find that more money is not the answer, we come to realize that in many ways it can make things worse. Indeed, it's hard not to feel that something is terribly amiss when we hear stories about housing prices and rents so high in some Silicon Valley towns that full-time workers earning $50,000 a year there have to be put up in homeless shelters.

Whether or not we want to be wealthy, we can all agree that there is a certain cosmic folly in obsessing about bigger houses and faster cars and shinier baubles. And so a new American dream is taking shape. It's still about making it, but with less not with more. Those who don't aspire to a big material footprint are no longer out of step, but rather, are setting the pace for the rest of us. MATERIALISM—JWS

92

THE PURSUIT OF HAPPINESS

*Happiness in this world, when it comes, comes incidentally.
Make it the object of pursuit, and it leads us on a wild goose
chase, and is never attained. Follow some other object, and very
possibly we may find that we have caught happiness without
dreaming of it.*—Nathaniel Hawthorne

As Andrew Delbanco provocatively suggests, "The happiness business . . . has been a big business at least since Thomas Jefferson dropped the final term from John Locke's enumeration of human rights—'life, liberty, and . . . property'—and replaced it with what would become the motto of the new nation: 'the pursuit of happiness.'"

But Hawthorne is right. Happiness, when it comes, comes incidentally. Reflect on those moments that have brought you satisfaction over the last month. A job well accomplished. A friendship nurtured. The return of a child's hug. The motivation for each has not been a happy life, but a life well lived. Happiness is a by-product.

REPOSE—RKJ

93

A QUIET INTERSECTION

Suddenly, it's okay to discuss God at work. As many as 10,000 prayer groups in workplaces meet regularly. Over 80 conferences are held each year on spirituality and the workplace, up from just one a few years ago.

The best place to escape the stressful crush and crowding in a busy airport is not a bar or a shop or an airline club. It's the interfaith chapel. Usually tucked away down a seldom-used corridor, little known to and little used by other travelers, the interfaith chapel is my secret refuge in airports all over the country. The chapel is always a small, quiet, softly lighted place to sit and meditate or read. Each chapel is variously furnished and stocked with spiritual readings. Religion per se is a low-key element, no doubt because the chapel must accommodate people of many faiths, but this understatement works to great effect. It creates a hushed, soothing atmosphere of peace and tranquility that is barely broken by the periodic arrival and departure of the few other people who come in to take a moment to rest and pray. I usually stay longer than most, leaving at the last possible moment to catch my flight.

I don't do any work when I'm in one of these chapels. Rather, I catch my breath and recharge my batteries so that I can be ready for work when it's time to go. This is no different than the sort of break other travelers are trying to take in airport bars and shops and clubs, but I find those places to be just as crowded and stressful as the concourses and gates. The only place that truly offers me a brief respite to regroup is the one place in the airport where religion and spirituality intersect with business and commerce.

As we spend an ever greater portion of our lives at the office, our need to ensure some balance at work rises as well. Religion is the root source for much of the balance we want to create in our lives, hence it's no surprise that we see an increasingly visible presence of religion in the workplace. Religion comes to where people are, and the office is where more and more of us are more and more of the time. As we pursue our selfish economic interests in marketplace transactions, it is the selflessness at the core of religion that keeps us connected to the broader meanings and purposes of what we do and that create the true satisfactions in our lives. The desire for this kind of balance is one reason many people now drive around sporting the new bumper sticker that reads, "Real Success Is Ending Up In Heaven." Such a conjunction of work and religion can facilitate balance, just as for me, on a smaller scale, the interfaith chapels in the airports where I spend so much of my time offer me a chance to find focus and renewal as I make my way through the complexities and demands of the business day.   REPOSE—JWS

94

TIME ALONE

In a national survey commissioned by the Wall Street Journal and NBC News, 31 percent wished for more time alone; only 6 percent wished for less.

It sounds so vain—that we like ourselves straight up as much as this. But a little self-indulgence can do us good sometimes. Jesus wandered the desert alone for forty days, from which he returned with a reborn focus and faithfulness. Our time alone, too, can have this power of renewal and recommitment. But in our daily lives, we don't get much of a chance for this anymore. Everything around us tugs at us, seeking our attention, soliciting our involvement, separating us from ourselves.

Ten years ago my morning commute was twenty minutes of time to myself. I had time to reflect on the day ahead or just to let my thoughts meander a bit before I'd have to line them up in lockstep at the office. Today my morning commute is a crowded tangle of aggravated drivers, construction detours, and roadside signs screaming to get my notice. That small piece of my day that I used to have for myself has been lost, converted into yet more time that I spend wrangling with others. My commute has become so demanding that it's dangerous for me to let my own thoughts get between me and the road. In losing a bit of time to myself, I get to the office feeling agitated instead of refreshed. And often enough, that starts the day off with a sour taste.

So I have built a brief pause into my morning once I arrive at the office in order to collect myself before I get started with my workday. For me to do my best for others, I need some space to revitalize the best in myself. I can take care of others only if I have first taken care of myself. Time alone is not just about vanity or about what I can take for myself. It's about being able to give something back to others too.

REPOSE—JWS

95

FORTY WINKS

The Epworth Sleepiness Scale is widely used to measure sleep deprivation. This scale asks how likely you are to fall asleep in situations ranging from reading to watching TV to talking with friends to sitting in a public place to being in a car. The harder you find it to stay awake in these situations, the more you suffer from sleep deprivation. Indeed, even just a slight to moderate chance of falling asleep in every one of the situations asked about, adds up to sleep deprivation worth worrying about.

I added up my score on the Epworth scale and concluded that I probably should have been getting some shut eye instead of taking the time to answer those questions. One thing I did notice about the Epworth scale, though, is that all of the situations included are ones in which we're sitting down. I guess that means if we go to sleep standing up, we automatically flunk! The real issue in this test seems to be whether or not we can stay awake while sitting up.

I taught a lot of introductory undergraduate classes while I was a graduate student. And one thing I learned was that no matter how many students doze off or leave the room or do something else, you just ignore it and keep right on going to the next overhead transparency. This means that today negative feedback no longer has any impact on me. Whatever happens in whatever I do, I just ignore it and keep right on going.

In a similar way, we've all become so accustomed to the sleep deprivation etched into the tired faces of those around us that we just ignore it. We no longer think it odd that when people sit, they're soon out like a light. Ourselves included. Sitting and staying awake at the same time is today's trick feat of coordination. Do we regret what we miss? Do we worry that as we sit and doze, life is passing us by? Do we fret that while sleeping, we might have lost a once in a lifetime chance to see or do something? Well, probably. But the problem is, by and large, we're at a point where we're simply going to ignore this negative feedback and just grab a quick snatch of sleep, whenever and wherever we can. Perhaps we need to see the sleep deprivation problem presented to us in a way that will make us sit up and pay attention, say, by scoring ourselves not on the sleep we've lost but on what we've lost by living a life in which sleep loss is taken for granted.   REPOSE—JWS

96
LET'S DO LUNCH

A survey in 1996 found that 39 percent of us no longer take a real lunch break. Another survey in 1997 found that 55 percent of workers take 15 minutes or less for lunch. And another 1996 survey discovered as few as 12 percent of workers take an hour or more to eat lunch.

More and more, it better fit in one hand or we're not going to eat it. We eat on the fly, especially during the work week. We don't really break for lunch anymore, we just sort of take a break around lunchtime—during which we check voice mail, check e-mail, sort regular mail, return phone calls, debrief from the last meeting, check our slides for the next meeting, look over our schedule for the rest of the day, and last but not least, eat. But in missing lunch, do we wind up missing it? That is, does this matter to us? Taking lunch has always been a sort of ritual bonding among business people—more about socializing than dining, more about the meeting than the eating. What we've lost in the crush to get things done at work is less a meal than an opportunity for social connection. Hungry for success, we starve our relationships.

What we need, perhaps, is not so much lunch per se as it is putting a little lunch hour, so to speak, back into our lives. My first job was close to the apartment where my wife Joy and I lived. Everyday, I came home for lunch. It was a quick bite over which Joy and I could share our days and catch up. But as my work schedule got busier, particularly my travel, I quit coming home for lunch. As the years went by, we began to miss that small bit of time we'd had to ourselves. We felt we'd lost something that was special and close. Recently, we resolved to recover what we'd lost, although not by meeting at home for lunch. The opportunity for having lunch together at home had long since passed. Instead, we now make a date one night every week. Once arranged, this date is unbreakable. We organize our schedules around it and we use the time on our date to share our days and catch up. It's not lunch, but it's a sort of "lunch hour" that we've put back into our lives. It feeds something vital in our relationship the way we fed it and nourished it so many years ago.   REPOSE—JWS

97
A NEW PERSPECTIVE

Pearl Buck was asked if she would like to be young again? "No," she said, "for I have learned too much to wish to lose it."

In our throw-away culture, young is often thought to be better. Computers are but the most obvious of examples. My three-year old laptop is a dinosaur, almost incapable of keeping up. But in life, a different pattern emerges. With aging comes the possibility of choosing what brings us satisfaction, of relaxing our defenses and learning how to pick our battles, of rediscovering relationships, of being more candid with those we care about. In old age, we are released to be who we want to be rather than simply working to fulfill others' satisfactions.

"Carpe Diem"! Seize the day! This does not mean ignoring the past, but "re-membering" it—putting it into a new and more integrated perspective. To "re-member" is to look back in experience and to see life according to new patterns and values. Rather than rue our retirement, some find in aging a richness that allows both present and future to gain in significance.   WONDER—RKJ

98
IN HARMONY WITH THE WHOLE

The best of artists never make a creation that is not hid in the stone, in marble fixed, and yet the work is done by hand, which follows mind and meditation.—Michelangelo

The sculptor exercises his craft freely, without constraint, but always in harmony with what the stone calls forth.

Think of the jazz musician who improvises freely, but always on the melody. Similarly, the architect must fit landscape and building together into a harmonious whole. Building alone is not enough. There is, in many of the arts, a relationship established between the work and its medium that is aesthetic, almost spiritual. But such aesthetics is not limited to the arts.

My father owns a structural engineering firm. The work is largely analytical in nature, and yet Dad speaks of looking at a set of drawings and being able to visualize whether the design works or not. It is an aesthetic judgment, one that asks how fitting is the design. Executives, too, often visualize a solution to a problem before being able to spell out all the steps analytically. That comes later. Similarly, scientists. Work "works" best when it is seen as part of a bigger whole. Michelangelo was right. Mind and meditation are to precede and guide our work. WONDER—RKJ

99

THE VIEW FROM NANKOWEAP

The Colorado River in its relentless flow has carved the Grand Canyon and will continue to shape it throughout time. The Grand Canyon has been formed by what David Brower famously called, "Time and the river flowing." In 1903, Theodore Roosevelt reflected on the marvel and natural beauty of the Grand Canyon and asked that it be left alone. He did not think that mere men could improve the work of the ages.

Several times I have stood alongside the ancient Anasazi granaries hidden in the cliff face five hundred feet above the Nankoweap delta of the Grand Canyon, listening to guides employ the vernacular of science to explain the location of these granaries in terms of protection from exposure and enemies. As I've listened, my eye has always wandered to the distant view of the Colorado River as it makes a grand, panoramic sweep around Nankoweap to go roaring away into the wee distance downriver. It's a magnificent vista, with the power of a cathedral to inspire a sense of the sublime.

This is an experience we've all had, for we've all been to places like this—places that put things in perspective, reminding us of what we tend to overlook in the hustle and bustle of the day to day. Indeed, I've always thought, standing there at Nankoweap, that the real reason the Anasazi came up here to work and live was no different than ours. And our reason is pretty straightforward: we just plain ol' like the view.

When life looks this good, we feel good about life. When we see life spread out before us in such a grand and glorious way, our own lives feel grand and glorious. But we must look up from our work and look out into life in order to see this kind of majesty. That's what the Grand Canyon does for me, and that is why I return again and again. I want to hike up to those granaries and take in the view yet one more time.

WONDER—JWS

100

EVERY LITTLE BIT COUNTS

Many people remain apathetic for fear that their actions won't make a difference in a culture deeply attached to materialism and competition. But if all Americans remain inactive out of this sense of defeat, the collective effect will be devastating.

If I see a nail lying in the road when I'm running, I'll stop and pick it up. It's not much, but I'm convinced it's a small thing worth doing. I've had my share of flat tires from running over them. About once a week, I see one and I pick it up. Sometimes I'll joke to my friends about the source of all of these nails. Maybe our homes and offices are gradually coming apart, one nail at a time. Maybe squirrels find them and drop them in the road when they realize the nails are inedible. Maybe it's some kind of underground prank known only to a few people. But all kidding aside, I think it's most likely that nails just don't seem important enough to worry about, so we let them fall where they may. Being this slipshod with nails bothers me, though, because I like an obstacle-free road. It reduces some of the unexpected work that often plagues us when we're trying to get around in life. Just think, for example, how clean and safe our roads would be if we all made a point of picking up loose nails. So I always stop and pick up the nails in the belief that small things matter, that, indeed, small things can often make the biggest difference in the grand scheme of things. NURTURE—JWS

101
COMING HOME

In a survey commissioned by the American Animal Hospital Association, 57 percent of pet owners preferred to be stranded on a desert island with their pet than with another person. Medical research finds pet owners to be healthier, prompting some insurers to offer lower rates to people with pets.

When the company he worked for was sold to a competitor, a friend of mine, Greg, was relocated from his hometown to a big city far away. He did okay—big promotion, more pay, new opportunities with a much bigger company. But he and his family never felt at home in this new city, and they looked forward to the day when the right chance to move back would come along. That happened a few years later as his company went through another major transition.

Greg and I sat around one afternoon talking about his move back. He described how he'd hit the road packed to the gills, determined to drive through the night to get home, only to make a sudden U-turn at the on ramp to the interstate. Back at his house, he went to the spot in his backyard where, just about a year before, he'd buried his dog. She had been a merry old dog, a great joy to be around. A miniature mutt, half-mad in her sheer, hyperkinetic exhilaration from being in your company, she always skittered into a room with her short legs a blur of motion. She was nonstop, with boundless energy—and part of my friend's household for seventeen years. That afternoon, before my friend could leave the city he'd endured, before he could go home to the town he'd missed, he dug up his dog's remains, which had been carefully packed in a sealed box, and placed them in the back seat of his car to be reinterred in the familiar back yard to which he and his family returned. Greg said to me, only somewhat tongue-in-cheek, "I hated that city so much, I couldn't even bear to leave my dead dog behind in it!"

He still tells this story like that, but you sense beneath all of the tough-guy bravado that it's a story less about the town than the dog. Going home was as much about what he brought back with him as what he came back to. Indeed, he just loved that dog too much not to take her back with him because it never could have felt like home without her there too.

NURTURE—JWS

102
A RICHLY TEXTURED LIFE

From 1990 to 1996, 1.8 million people moved to rural areas, far more than the 1.4 million who moved away in the eighties. This reversal led to the highest rural growth rates observed in decades.

It's not the farms but the farmland that we're after when we head back to the country. We want bucolic as long as it's not too rustic. We're not returning to live off the land.

Instead, we're looking for a place that can restore some texture and charm and stimulation to our lives—a more intricate mosaic of satisfactions; less of the bland monotony of look-alike superhighways and strip malls. So we're revisiting old ground. But this is not about rural living per se. City planners are also anticipating a boom in in-town living.

One artist friend of mine moved his studio from the outskirts of a big city to ten acres of high plains desert out west. He raves over it for the view, the hikes, the climbing, the wildlife, the whitewater nearby, and the extremes of weather. Another friend of mine just moved from the 'burbs to a renovated walk up in the center-city. He raves about it for the sidewalks, the restaurants, the nightlife, the neon, the density and variety of people, and the electricity of nonstop activity.

What each of my friends describes, one from way downtown and the other from way out of town, is exactly the same thing—a texture and a density to life that had been missing in their old haunts and routines. Sure, they're taking some risks. And both have given up a few conveniences and creature comforts, but nothing vital and certainly nothing that was a salve for their souls. They've left behind what was nice to have to immerse themselves head to toe in what they have to have. NURTURE—JWS

103

UNREHEARSED

At a wedding we recently attended, the bride and groom had their service videotaped. Then the "movie" was premiered at their reception to applause. The camera people sometimes had to stand in front of the wedding party during the service, but people pretended not to mind. After all, the event was just the set-up for the movie that followed and which would be a lifetime keepsake!

Is this a metaphor for how we too often live? Are we at risk of confusing the performance with a taping? Such is Neal Gabler's thesis in his book, *Life: The Movie*. He chronicles how we are increasingly turning our lives into a movie that we work at continually. We let Martha Stewart be our set designer creating our "look" at home. Ralph Lauren is our costumer. We want to be sure we have gotten it right.

But we know life is not a meant to be a rehearsal! It is not a taping of a movie to be played later. Mozart is said to have sat at the piano playing new compositions by the hour, which he never wrote down. "Tragic," some would say. I would say, "Wondrous."

NURTURE—RKJ

104

WAKE UP!

Research shows that 63 million Americans are sleep-deprived and that 23 percent of adults report having fallen asleep at the wheel within the past year. Some studies conclude that sleepy drivers cause as many accidents as drunk drivers.

Wake up! This is scary! Enough to keep one up at night. Enough to keep you wide awake at the wheel, trying to avoid being hit by all of the other sleepyheads out there. It's an eye-opener to think that for at least one-quarter of us being in our cars and fighting traffic is the most relaxing place we find ourselves during the day. If we can't find some way to get a little sleep, we may well be headed for the big sleep. At the very least, it's likely that we will see a new approach to public safety. What will it be? Will state legislatures make driving-while-drowsy a moving violation? Will the highway patrol give droopy-eyed drivers field tests for wakefulness? Will violators be hauled off to jail to sleep it off? However it comes about, though, sooner or later, we must wake up to the fact that sleep deprivation is a serious threat on our highways, and even more importantly, in our lives as well.

NURTURE—JWS

105
CHASING HAPPINESS

As people spin faster and faster in the pursuit of merely personal happiness, they become exhausted in the futile effort of chasing themselves.—Andrew Delbanco

When my daughter Margi was a year old, she got a string with a toy attached caught on her diaper. Crawling around a central stairwell in our house, she saw the toy up ahead of her but could never reach it because it moved forward as she moved. She ended up "chasing her tail" until she got too tired to continue. We often laugh about this as a family.

Margi's experience is a metaphor for some of our lives, as Andrew Delbanco has recognized. I am reminded of the writer of Ecclesiastes who saw the futility of chasing after ourselves and after our own happiness. Just as with my baby daughter, it simply wears you out. In this Old Testament book, the author assumed the persona of King Solomon and narrated how he built houses and planted vineyards, made himself pools, and gathered much gold and silver. "Whatever my eyes desired I did not keep from them," he relates. But he also concludes, "Then I considered all that my hands had done . . . and again, all was vanity and a chasing after wind." (Ecclesiastes 2:10–11 *NRSV*)

This ancient Hebrew sage is blunt in his criticism of our chase after happiness. But he also suggests an alternate strategy for life, one that brings joy as a by-product. Rather than leave his readers to laugh cynically, he calls us to step back from our self-serving efforts and instead enjoy the gift of life as it unfolds. "There is nothing better for mortals," he instructs, "than to eat and drink, and find enjoyment in their toil." (Ecclesiastes 2:24 *NRSV*)

We need not spin faster and faster to create joy. Instead, we can receive life as the divine gift it is.   HAPPINESS—RKJ

106
THE PRICE OF PERFECTION

An analysis of liposuction surgeries found one reported death for every 5,224 procedures.

Cosmetic (or to use the more highbrow term, "aesthetic") surgery is an explosive growth industry. When our work-outs at our health clubs don't do the trick, there are more and more alternatives. Cosmetic procedures by board-certified doctors mushroomed to over one million surgeries in 1998. Since 1992, there has been an increase of 328 percent in surgeries to lift buttocks, 102 percent for eyelids, 172 percent for foreheads, 270 percent for thighs, 347 percent for upper arms, and 177 percent for tummy tucks. Liposuction, the most popular cosmetic surgery, increased from 47,212 to 172,079 procedures.

Here, surely, is a beauty that is only skin deep. Why not put the money to alternate uses such as a massage once a

■ ■ 162 ■ ■

month, or replanting your backyard garden, or even supporting a malnourished child in another part of the world? Peace, not perfection, will prove a more satisfying goal.

HAPPINESS—RKJ

107

FAMOUSLY OBSCURE

Many public figures misgauge their own celebrity. The awards and recognition showered upon them are not an indication of love or personal regard. Instead, this attention usually reflects nothing more than the passing fancy of public opinion at that particular moment.

As an undergraduate, I used to thumb rides on the weekends to visit my girlfriend one hundred miles away. Late one fall semester, I was headed back on a Sunday afternoon and was standing alongside the last stretch of highway into campus with my thumb out. A robin's-egg-blue muscle car pulled off and I piled in. The driver introduced himself and seemed to expect me to recognize his name, but I didn't. An uncomfortable silence ensued, so I scrambled for something complimentary to say. "Nice car" was what I came up with, which didn't help. More silence. I tried again. "Where do you live on campus?" He named the dorm, which I recognized as the one where the basketball team was housed. So I figured we could talk about that. "Wow. That's the dorm where the basketball team lives." Oh yes, he told me. In fact, he played on the basketball team. Ah, finally, I thought, some common ground—me and him, fellow extracurricularites. Overly eager, I brought that to his attention. "Really. That's great. You know, I'm on the debate team." This time, a deep silence—along with a funny look on his face. I rallied for one last try. "Do you play varsity or jayvee?" He turned to me with a crooked smile, half-impatience, half-smirk, and said he thought he'd probably be playing varsity this year.

That's when the light bulb went on. This guy was our big-name freshman recruit and here I was in his car telling him I was on the debate team! At that point, I exclaimed my recognition of him after which we chatted nonstop about the coming season for the last few miles into campus. He went on to a fabulous career, college and pro. But these days his name is lost among the pantheon of other big-name stars who have come and gone over the years, all of them, famously obscure.

I used to tell this story to bring some attention to me based on his celebrity status, but that didn't last long. His celebrity doesn't have much clout anymore. Now I tell this story just for myself. It reminds me that celebrity is nothing but something manipulated by the media to sell magazines and movies, and that life has given me my own ride, which, all in all, has gone famously well. HAPPINESS—JWS

108

GOOD WORKS

Studies of lottery winners show that they are no happier a year after winning than they were before winning.

The opposite is true too. Those who have suffered a major accident or trauma are no less happy afterward than before. Researchers calculate that about half of what accounts for how happy we are is in our genes. Try as we might, we can only make ourselves so much happier or, for that matter, so much unhappier. That puts the pleasure principle in perspective. If happiness is what we use as our road map in deciding where to go and what direction to take, then we'll only get so far. The feel-good philosophy of limitless leisure is, in fact, limited in the extent to which it can point us toward a life we can really feel good about. We wind up frustrated because, time and again, we find that even after we accomplish things we think are going to make us happier, we continue to feel much the same as always. This doesn't mean that we should court unhappiness or resign ourselves to utterly unacceptable things that we could change. It's just that we need to be reasonable in making decisions about where we're headed.

A friend of mine quit his job as a high-powered management consultant to move to the mountains and work part time as a business writer. He thought he'd finally be able to escape all the irritants in his life. However, I've noticed that he complains no less with time on his hands than he did with not a minute to spare. In his extra time, though, he has organized a network of retired executives who volunteer as mentors to local entrepreneurs just starting businesses in the community. And it's the time he works on this extra activity more than his extra leisure time that gives him the greatest satisfaction, even as he continues to grumble and grouse about life in general. It's the do-good things more than the feel-good things that keep our lives from detouring down a dead end.

HAPPINESS—JWS

109
PLANTING GARDENIAS BY THE DOZENS

A devout life does bring wealth, but it's the rich simplicity
of being yourself before God. Since we entered the world
penniless and will leave it penniless, if we have bread on
the table and shoes on our feet, that's enough.
—St. Paul (1 Timothy 6:9 (The Message))

My friend Stuart, a medical doctor, refuses to schedule himself for more than what other doctors consider half a practice. As a result he earns one-half the typical doctor's salary, but his life is rich and full. After Stuart completed his studies at Tulane and Emory, he moved to a mid-sized town in Kentucky in order to escape the rat race. He didn't want to pay high rates for insurance, and he also didn't want to raise his family amid the hectic pace of the big city. He bought a small gentleman's farm and planted gardenias by the dozens, spent time talking with his patients—the first time I visited him, I had laryngitis, but he wanted to discuss Plato—read philosophy and theology, got involved in his local church, and coached his daughter's soccer team. He also was a superb general practitioner.

As a doctor, Stuart's salary is still more than adequate. He has far more than the minimum alluded to by St. Paul. Nevertheless, he has made what many would consider a radical choice. He has opted to live more simply and to work at a measured pace, and as a result his life is more humane. It takes courage to make such choices, but the results pay huge dividends. HAPPINESS—RKJ

110
THE FAMILY TASTE TEST

The news that Brenda Barnes was stepping down as president and chief executive of Pepsi-Cola North America to spend more time with her family was big news in corporate America. Years of long hours and travel had finally caught up. For Brenda, the trade-offs weren't worth the reward any longer.

Family won this taste test—as it does for many of us these days. Work to the exclusion of all else is getting harder and harder to swallow. Life is the sort of challenge we want to take on. This case is a high-profile instance of a broad shift that's at work nowadays. Many of the talented, accomplished women who reinvented the workplace are now reinventing the definition of success.

Success is being redefined in terms of the breadth and intrinsic worth of our priorities, a change that reaches beyond the workplace. This means that success is being measured not only by what we've achieved but by what we've sacrificed as well. The bigger the sacrifice in our lives, the less successful we are in the way we work. So we can leave a big job behind and still be regarded as successful. Status is tied less and less to what we have and more and more to what we've given up—which is why women are leading this new definition of success, for the gains women have made have been much harder won with much greater sacrifice along the way.

My sister is one such success—and a role model for me. She started her career as a programmer, and moved up rapidly to become a systems analyst and then a senior consultant. She was headed even higher when, one year, she reached a point where she had to decide whether she was going to put more time into work or into family. Her girls had reached an age at which they could benefit from more of her attention, and so to get the time and flexibility she needed to do that, she voluntarily moved back into programming. I don't know if I could be as courageous as that. What I learned from my sister was that success comes in many flavors, not all of which make work the primary ingredient. HAPPINESS—JWS

111

A SUMMER LESSON

Summer is different. We've learned from years of living by the school calendar that summer proceeds at a more relaxed pace. In the workplace, we see this lifelong conditioning show up in summer hours and long weekends, in rush hours that begin later in the mornings and earlier in the afternoons, and in many other changes that we make in how we do business in order to accommodate the shift in how we live life.

Why can't we live like it's summer all year long? We needn't do less, just do everything, if not more, at a lesser pace. It requires that we take a step back and ask ourselves whether we push and shove for any purpose other than that of the furious pace itself. Is there a reason to barrel through revolving doors or rush onto elevators as soon as the doors open or roll through stop signs and tollbooths or crowd closely behind those ahead of us in line? Surely we can add some ebb to the flow of our day without falling behind.

There are places, of course, where it never feels like summer—in particular, the hourly shuttles a few airlines run between high-traffic cities. Year-round, these flights are an incessant push and shove. Passengers rush on board, cram in hurried, last-second phone calls, gulp down a snack and a drink in the air, crowd the aisles to get out, and then charge off both ends of the plane. Shuttle gates are laid out to accommodate people with no time to waste, people who are always on a last-minute schedule, people in a furious, no-nonsense boil. This frenzied, self-absorbed, commercial pace is what shuttle flights are all about.

But what do we want for our own lives? Summer or shuttle? At the very least, there's got to be a happy medium somewhere between these two extremes. Even though we know that life can never be an endless summer, neither should it be an endless shuttle.

After spending years working at a shuttle-like pace, I finally crashed and burned out on it. Nowadays, I approach work very differently. And it turns out that even at a more relaxed pace, I always get to where I'm going no later than I ever got there before. I've come to see that the furious hustle I used to maintain was subjecting me to the worry and stress of false deadlines. Having realized that, I've begun to carry this more relaxed approach even further. Now I pause as I enter buildings to hold the door a moment for those a few steps behind me. I allow not one but two cars at a time to pull ahead of me in a traffic jam. I even go the long way home on occasion just to take in the view. My work is no less serious than before, but the feel of my work is much more satisfying because I've found a happy medium that gives me a better balance between work and life.   AUTHENTICITY—JWS

112
DOING WHAT WE SAY

Americans value themselves primarily through who they are at home—not what they do on the job.—Alan Wolfe

At least we say we value ourselves primarily by who we are at home. Yet increasingly, we contradict our words by what we do. We say to pollsters that if given three extra hours each day, we would spend these with our families and friends. But there is cause to wonder. Many of us look to our work for our amusement as well as for our livelihood. And thanks to technology, the workplace is everywhere, even where we don't want it (e.g., the concert, the bedroom, the restaurant). Some of us work as much as we do because we think we will then be able to retire early and spend more time with spouse and children. But we risk abandoning what we say we cherish most. Just saying "No" should refer to other things besides drugs.

AUTHENTICITY—RKJ

113
BRINGING WORK HOME

Nationwide surveys by Yankelovich have asked women:
"Do you agree or disagree that having a child is an
experience every woman should have?"
Boomer women in 1979 . . . 45% agreed
GenXer women in 1998 . . . 68% agreed

Boomer women broke new ground in the workplace, but not without paying a price. Striking a balance between work and family, for example, often meant putting family off, or at least second. Family had to fit the demands of work. For example, on-site day care, one of the rallying cries of the eighties, is exactly that sort of a solution, one that's about bringing home to the office. The emphasis is different today. Now we hear more about telecommuting and flextime, solutions rooted in bringing work home. Because of the strides made by boomers, young women today can aspire to even greater success with fewer family sacrifices. Today's young women were often the children of single-parent homes, blended households, or latchkey lifestyles—something that they want to avoid for their families. Not that they want to give up any freedoms or choices, mind you. They're going to pioneer the next frontier of work styles in order to fully accommodate a life. Indeed, we will all fall in behind these women as they show us better ways to balance work and life, for the presumption that work at any cost comes first is being replaced by a recognition that work no matter the cost is not much of an accomplishment.   AUTHENTICITY—JWS

114

BUILT ON ROCK

Change based on principle is progress. Constant change without principle becomes chaos.—Dwight D. Eisenhower

I get away on a commercial river trip with the Grand Canyon Dories every other year or so. One of the guides asked me once why I keep coming back. She was curious to know if the canyon experience touched or nurtured or perhaps even revealed something she referred to as "the truest part" of me. I was stumped. I'd never thought about it in that way before, and upon reflection, I was taken aback to realize how hard it is for me to point to the truest part of myself. I think this is a challenge for many of us nowadays. More and more, we're forced to be many selves because, increasingly, our lives are jump-cuts from role to role, situation to situation, and setting to setting, each separate, compartmentalized, and discrete. Like performers with multiple roles in some elaborate stage production, we keep changing back and forth to fit the choreography of the moment as we're pulled along from scene to scene.

What, then, is the truest part of our selves? Is there some defining principle or core element we can rely upon to move us forward and keep us progressing? Or is there nothing but the chaos of nonstop shifting and changing? A common workday for me is to awaken at home, fly to another city, hustle through a series of meetings, then finish up overnight somewhere else, ready for the next day's jumble of changing venues and locales. I wear many hats as I weave my way through the workaday web of things to do, people to see, places to go. Sometimes I'll look around in a conference room or a hotel lobby and feel utterly disconnected from where I started out that morning, where I was just a short while ago, and where I'm headed next. Each situation is a setting wholly unto itself. In which situation am I truest to myself? What principle or sense of my true self can I use to keep me on track and steer me toward progress, growth, and fulfillment?

We all want to ground our lives in something solid and true like the house Jesus commended to us, built on rock, secure from the rains and the winds and the floods. I guess I've just taken that a bit too literally in my many journeys through the stone corridors of the Grand Canyon. I am always inspired and revitalized by its power, its quietude, and its sanctuary, even though I can't say for sure exactly what it touches deep inside me. I try to carry this sensibility with me at work, whereas I leave work behind when I'm in the canyon—which surely means that the Grand Canyon does, in fact, affect some part of my truest self. The pageantry of the canyon is a spectacular reminder that life is a sublime affair, extraordinary, mysterious, and majestic. This is a canyon so grand that even from its depths I can see and marvel at the grandeur of life itself.

In my constant, day-to-day donning and doffing of various personae like some overactive chameleon, the memory of the Grand Canyon helps get me through. I've come to believe that this sense of wonder is not a luxury but an essential requirement, indeed, a core principle, for living a life that can transcend, at least occasionally, all that is dreary and trifling, banal and stale, all that rides us and works us down. What I take away from the canyon experience is exactly what I need, if not what we all need from some such touchstone—which is much more than just a life that is not work, it is a life that just simply works.

AUTHENTICITY—JWS

115

CHANGING TO STAY THE SAME

Work completed by the Families and Work Institute shows that one of the strongest predictors of whether a company has work-life assistance programs is the percentage of women holding top executive positions.

All the old ways of doing things are in flux. Change is so thick and powerful nowadays that you can almost smell it in the air. New sorts of people are taking charge. Women have begun to top the corporate ladder, and this is just the tip of the iceberg. Young girls are getting more education nowadays than young boys. Hispanics lead year-to-year population growth, such that America is on its way to being the second largest Latin nation in the world. Twenty-somethings led the dot-com revolution and the teens behind them will do the same for wireless. Baby boomers are refusing to concede any ground to age or retirement. Immigrants have taken up the work that keeps America functioning.

All around us these days, the people we see making the biggest differences in how we live and work are not the same kinds of people we remember doing so in the past. With little fanfare, new ways of doing things are being put in place by these new leaders, and in many cases, the values we cherish most are better championed and supported as a result. This is what we see in the kinds of findings reported by the Families and Work Institute about the sorts of business leaders most likely to put programs in place to help employees balance their jobs with their families. Indeed, when we look closely, we often find that the most important part of change is what's constant about it. Not infrequently, doing something differently is the only way to sustain what we most want to keep.

In this regard, I think of the few old friends I've been able to keep up with over the years. The differences between how we used to be and how we are today make up a running joke among us, and every time we get together we add a new punch line to that joke as we tease each other about "hot-rodding" in our minivans or shagging to the beat of the washing machine or insisting that gray is actually dirty blonde. Each of us has changed a lot over the years, but it's precisely because of that that we've been able to stay friends for so long. Our friendship doesn't get stale. What we have remains fresh and smart, interesting and vital, exciting and compelling. For many reasons, we simply would've lost what we had years ago if we hadn't allowed it to change, not the least of which is that it wouldn't have taken too long before we ran out things to talk about! Change has been the agency of constancy for us. The more our lives have taken different paths, the closer we've come together and the better our friendship has become. Only by updating ourselves have we been able to stay friends. And so, too, I think, for everything that means something to us. Only by changing is it able to last. AUTHENTICITY—JWS

116

DOING SOMETHING WITH OURSELVES

I'm a machine, says the spot-welder. I'm caged, says the bank teller. I'm a mule, says the steelworker. A monkey can do what I do, says the receptionist. I'm less than a farm implement, says the migrant worker. I'm an object, says the high-fashion model.—Studs Terkel

One of Terkel's interviewees explained that people are looking in their work for a calling, not just a job. The Latin word for such a "calling" is *vocatio*, from which comes the word vocation. Too often we have equated our vocation with our job. But it is more than that. Our vocation is what we do with our job. Spot-welding and high-fashion modeling can be either a job or a calling. It depends on whether we can bring to it any purpose or value beyond itself. AUTHENTICITY—RKJ

117

ALL OVER WITH THE SHOUTING

Major league baseball umpire Larry Young noted once that ref-
ereeing Special Olympics basketball in his off-season is unlike
anything else he's encountered in sports. Rather than the shout-
ing and yelling he has to put up with in other kinds of leagues,
Special Olympics players hug him after the game.

I used to push for every edge and every advantage.
Verbal terrorism was my favorite tool of intimidation. One
of my clients used to be a major airline, and after a particularly rocky start on one of its Monday morning flights,
I complained in no uncertain way on the 800-line. The
next day, my client contact called to inquire about what
had gone on. I was surprised she was even aware I'd had a
problem, so I asked how she'd known. She said I had been
flagged in their database as having been verbally abusive
on that call. I was dumbfounded, for I'd made a special
point of not cursing or raising my voice. Apparently, I'd
been singled out for other reasons—my impatience, my
tone of voice, my sarcasm. It caused me to rethink how I

came across to others. I saw that flexing muscle can be just as hurtful as actually throwing the punch. This was brought even closer to home when my wife went back to work. All of a sudden I was concerned that some customer would speak to her the way I'd spoken to other customer service agents in the past. It was only then that I realized that everyone I'd pushed around in the past had been somebody's wife or mother or sister.

So I started to take stock of myself, to appreciate what I have, and to accept that few people ever set out to do the wrong thing. Getting angry is the wrong response to honest mistakes. My aggression was misdirected and counterproductive, eating away at me while failing to make anything better. I'd been doing nothing but sharing and passing along misery when I should have been planting the seeds of happiness and hope instead. Nowadays, whatever the situation—irrespective of who's in the right and no matter the outcome—I feel pretty rotten about myself if I make somebody cower and submit. I feel great only when I can make someone smile. INTEGRITY—JWS

118

GROUNDED

Come, let us build ourselves a city, and a tower with its top in the heavens, and let us make a name for ourselves.
—*Genesis 11:4 (NRSV)*

The biblical story of the tower of Babel describes the building of a tower "with its top in the heavens." What is pictured is an attempt to do something so great that it takes the builders beyond their human limitations. As a result, God judges their work idolatrous. These workers are like Icarus, who in Greek mythology flew too close to the sun with his hand-made wings and fell to his death when the wax melted. Whether sacred or secular, history records the continual temptation to try to be like God. Rather than serving others and the Other, these workers focus on promoting themselves. How easy it is to become self-focused and forget that our work is vocation, a calling.

INTEGRITY—RKJ

119

CHEATING OURSELVES

Businesses have reported a surprising byproduct of the prosperity of the new economy of the nineties: cheating. Not paying tolls, not paying restaurant bills, not paying to golf; just taking without paying. A sort of there-for-the-taking kind of attitude, born of a new, more aggressive set of expectations and sense of entitlement.

The mantra of the nineties boom was to "do what it takes to get what we want." Sometimes, though, we acted as if this meant we should "do whatever it takes." But these are not the same. Working hard and doing what it takes does not give us permission to break the rules and do whatever it takes. Yet more and more, even with the nineties behind us, we're on this slippery slope, where it's getting harder and harder to hold fast. We admire those who know how to get an edge on the competition. We want to do this ourselves. But when this is what we value most of all, we begin to lose respect for all else. Indeed, it seems that what offends us most about those who cut corners is that we've lost an edge to them. Whether or not they've crossed the line legally or morally is almost beside the point. Just look at how we wait in line nowadays. We don't wait patiently; we jockey for position and advantage. And when someone breaks in front of us, our reaction can get way out hand, way out of all proportion to the offense.

What are we to make of what we've become? Heavy business travelers like me make a point of keeping our edge on the road, which is directly related to the amount of travel we do. The more we travel, the better our edge in service, upgrades, and special offers. But why is it that so many heavy business travelers like me think that being forced to fly coach is almost too great a price to pay for more time off the road that could be spent with our families? Is a first-class seat that much better? Similarly, is the concierge floor in a hotel that much nicer or a bigger rental car that much roomier? Personally, I've come to think not. It seems to me that oftentimes, in reaching out to grab that little something extra, even when we do so playing by the rules, the people we wind up cheating the most are ourselves.   INTEGRITY—JWS

120
FUNNY BUSINESS

Making workplaces more fun is becoming a big business.
Humor consultants are being hired by many Fortune 500
companies to remake their working environments so that
workplaces are more relaxed and more joyful.

How much fun can you possibly have at work? After all, as people like to say, that's why it's called work. Can we really tighten up our business performance by loosening up around the office? Well, apparently so. Studies on productivity show a "return on mirth" that falls straight to the bottom line. Creative ideas are the lifeblood of competitive advantage at every company, and creativity is best nurtured and rewarded in a friendly environment. Even so, for most companies it is hard to make the organizational shift to such a wholly new culture, so it is literally no joking matter to make humor a top priority. It comes down, then, to each of us. We must bring it in the door and invest our workplaces with more good humor, one smile at a time.

I used to approach staff meetings as a no-nonsense occasion to drill into my staff a total fidelity to high standards. As a result, our work was always a cut above the competition, but I was unaware of the psychic toll inflicted by my management style until the morning when a newspaper article showed up in my in-box. Forwarded to me anonymously, the article told the story of a manager being sued for harassment. The sender had circled a passage describing how this manager was purported to have punished a subordinate by forcing him to get down on his knees and crawl underneath a desk and sit there for the duration of the staff meeting. Sending me this article was a daring move by some member of my staff for it was the suggestion by implication that I was somewhere on the same side of the continuum as this manager. As I reread the article, I suddenly burst into laughter at the absolute absurdity of what was described in this article. And it made me realize that my staff wasn't looking for relief from high standards, only from me.

I carried this article to our next staff meeting and announced that we were going to start something new. I could feel the anxiety in the room. I said that in the future whenever I crossed the line pushing for high standards, I would be required to sit underneath the conference room table for the duration of our staff meetings. So, going forward it would be up to them to decide if my demands and criticisms fairly recognized their commitment and performance. With that said, I pinned the article to the bulletin board and plopped down in a chair. It took a second, but the absurdity the punishment I was proposing for myself slowly broke the tension and everyone laughed out loud. They realized I was figuratively down on one knee asking for a second chance.

Since that staff meeting, the quality of our work has gotten even better than before. People are more willing to take risks and to reach even higher because we can all laugh together about the quirks that go along with us in our common quest for success. Everyday, each of us brings a bit of good humor to the office which we share with one another and from which we weave an ever tighter web of dedication, teamwork, and growth.

121

A WORLDWIDE WHISTLE-STOP

A study conducted by researchers at Carnegie Mellon University found that greater use of the Internet was correlated with declines in family interactions, fewer social contacts, and increases in depression.

It's not hard to find yourself alone in a crowd, especially if the crowd is virtual. But lack of community isn't the fault of the Internet. It's simply a problem that the Internet brings into sharper focus. It's easy to broaden your social contacts on the Internet. We all know people who've done so—parents in touch with their kids at college, teens chatting online, grandparents e-mailing their grandchildren, hobbyists sharing tips, members of fan clubs passing on gossip, groups of specialists sharing information about their interests, and so forth.

The fact that so many of us use the Internet to increase our isolation instead of our interaction tells more about us than about the Internet. Any technology, simple or complex, can be used in this way, not just the Internet. For example, lots of heavy business travelers know that the simplest and best way to isolate yourself from having to talk to the person sitting next to you on a plane is not to fake a nap, it's to put on headphones. You don't have to plug them into anything. Having them on is all it takes to foil even the chattiest traveler.

Technology does not animate itself. We bring it to life in the service of our own purposes and priorities. So what's worrisome nowadays is not the essence of the Internet but the essence of the Internet user. When connection tops our priority list, we'll want community as well as convenience from the Internet. Then we will make it safe, intimate, and inclusive, our worldwide whistle-stop. COMMUNITY—JWS

122
ONLY ONE THING

There is need of only one thing.—Jesus (Luke 10: 42 NRSV)

The story of Jesus coming to Bethany to share a meal with Mary and Martha is justly famous. It teaches us something about our well-intentioned work. Martha retreats to the kitchen to prepare Jesus an elaborate meal. Mary chooses instead to sit and listen to him. In a culture in which women had little significance beyond the kitchen and the bedroom, Mary's action was radical indeed. Martha was not pleased and asked Jesus to tell Mary to help her in the kitchen. But Jesus responded, "There is need of only one thing." That is, being with me takes priority. A meal at a friend's should be the occasion for enjoyment and conversation, not just duty. Keep it simple.

COMMUNITY—RKJ

123
THE MAIN COURSE

Surveys show that the majority of American families uphold the tradition of sitting down to a family dinner five nights or more a week.

My diabetes was diagnosed my first year out of college. I spent a night in the local hospital to learn the mechanics of insulin shots and blood sugar monitoring and the next day I bought a book about diabetic diets. My dad drove up to help me for a few days and we talked things through, but it wasn't until a couple of weeks later that I was able to take a break from graduate school and go home for a visit. On the way, I thought about one of the luxuries I'd had growing up—my mother's cooking. We ate a sit-down breakfast every morning: eggs, bacon, grits, and biscuits most days; pancakes other days. Dinner was formal. We gathered, said grace, then dug into pot roasts or casseroles or baked hams, or, my absolute favorite, fried chicken. Desserts were pies and ice cream or caramel cake. Breakfast and dinner were always so sumptuous that no one in my family wanted to miss a meal, and so we were able to stay in touch as a family. Now, though, I wondered what our meals would be like given my dietary restrictions.

When I got home, my dad and I went to the grocery store to buy some of the foods I could eat, from which my mother carefully prepared a meal specifically tailored to my diet. It wasn't the fried chicken and caramel cake I remembered, of course. It was better. In fact, it was the best meal I've ever had, because at dinner that night, I realized for the first time that those meals my mother had cooked for all those years had been about the food only in passing. She had been nourishing us, not simply feeding us. She hadn't been running a restaurant; she'd been running a home. The food had been about love not taste. She'd fed us as well as she could and as well as she knew how, and now, for me, she was going to start from scratch and learn how to do it all over again. What better food is there than that? The main course at our meals had always been our family, with some taste and nutritional benefits on the side. However much taste and nutrition might have changed because of my diabetes, the main course was the same as ever. And that tasted great.   COMMUNITY—JWS

124
SAFETY IN NUMBERS

Dr. Lisa Berkman followed 7,000 people for nine years and found that people with weaker or no social ties were three times as likely to die.

Get out of the house and into the 'hood. You're better off there. Because there is, indeed, safety in numbers. Don't think you can go it alone and go as long, at least on aver-age, as those who set their course with a crowd. This crowd is not just any old rabble, of course, but a circle of kith and kin where you can find nurture and care. We're enlivened and animated by our associations and interactions with others, and when those juices get flowing, we just keep going.

It's no surprise then that we've started to reconnect in lots of new and interesting ways. Book clubs are booming to such an extent that some publishers now offer titles in book club editions. Talk radio yammers away up and down the dial. The Internet ties us together at light speed with instant messaging and chat rooms and Web rings. Road racers must now step aside to make room for so called penguin brigades of walkers who come along more for camaraderie and celebration than to set a personal best. Musicians are adding home concerts to their tour schedules as fans turn their living rooms into intimate performance spaces and sell a small number of tickets for one night stands. Poetry slams are reviving the communal experience of the spoken word. From support groups to coffee bars to volunteering to adult education programs, we're after contact and connection.

But we want our privacy and our individuality too. These freedoms and prerogatives have been too hard-won. So what we seek and what we are flocking to are communities that can accommodate, not sublimate, our free agency. This paradoxal mix is the new form of community, the new imperative for our combines and associations. This new form of community empowers individuals through the collective power of the group, promotes our independence, and facilitates our self-determination while at the same time absorbing us in the group interaction that enhances our health and overall well-being. As we maximize our individual private interests, we can also get the group contact that's in our best interest.   COMMUNITY—JWS

125

ENGAGED IN SPORTS

According to the Yankelovich Monitor survey, 40 percent of Americans are sports enthusiasts, i.e., they express themselves through engaging in sports or gain satisfaction from following sports.

According to polls by Yankelovich, sports enthusiasts are more apt than the other 60 percent of the population to watch movies and videos, have get-togethers with friends, play games, have holiday parties, and relax with people from work. They are also more likely to look for new and different places and things to do during their vacations, to want to spend time with friends, to want to learn something new, and to seek to fulfill their sense of adventure. Not to mention play sports.

Some think sports are a waste of time, particularly if you are not an active participant. The perception is that the value of sports is simply physical, just a mindless escape. But others know better. The sports event creates community and instills a sense of adventure in fans and

participants alike that extends well beyond the playing field. Even rooting for a team has its value. It helps one engage life with renewed intensity and encourages us to connect with our co-players. COMMUNITY—RKJ

126
TIME FOR FRIENDS

We value friends as much as ever, but we spend less time with our friends than ever before. It seems that work and family are the only commitments important enough to warrant time in our schedules. Combined with increasing travel, more entertainment options, and more opportunities to get away, the joy friends bring us is more and more absent from our lives.

Over half of all Americans wish they were more involved in their community and the people in their neighborhoods. It's a yearning to make friends and be friends. Women are often better at maintaining ongoing friendships, but we all are finding it more difficult today. Last fall my wife and I went to Nashville for a business conference. Rather than returning home immediately, we took

an additional two days to go to Bowling Green, Kentucky where I had previously lived. I wanted my wife to meet my friends. John and Emily Perkins sold me my first house and became surrogate grandparents to my girls. My family had shared weekly meals with Charles and Donna Bussey. Arvin and Corrie Vos were close friends at church and work. And yet, I had not seen them in over a decade. There just hadn't seemed to be time.

According to the Yankelovich Monitor® survey, 65 percent of Americans say they get a real sense of belonging or a sense of community from their old friends and 68 percent feel a real need to know more people whose outlook on life and sense of values are similar to their own. Surely this was my experience. Medical people support such desires, reporting that strong friendships reduce stress and promote health. My trip "home" reminded me how important friends are. Life is lived best in community. We have already planned to meet the Busseys this spring in Europe!   COMMUNITY—RKJ

127

KEEPING CONNECTED

The National Longitudinal Study on Adolescent Health found that a sense of connection at home as well as a sense of connection at school were the two conditions most protective of children's well-being. And that it was the perception of connection itself that was key, not any specific program or set of actions.

I had a challenging freshman year at college. For the first time, I was at the mercy of my own self-discipline, which wasn't very good back then. Plus, I didn't make friends easily. But with the friends I did make, I fell too readily into the pointless campus carousing of the early seventies. On top of all of that, I was an active collegiate debater, which meant long nights at the library every week and tournament travel two or three weekends a month.

Almost immediately, I felt too thinly stretched to cope, so I made plans to quit the debate team. My partner was furious and others on the squad were only slightly less annoyed, except for the graduate assistant who was help-

ing to coach the team that year. We talked one night for a couple of hours, with me near tears, about how out of place I felt on campus. As we wound down our talk, he encouraged me to stay on the team, but not because of anything to do with debating. He told me that the debate team, with its squad room and activities, its purpose and history, would give me a place on campus where I belonged. It would be a place I could come to each day and feel a part of something, a place that could connect me and plug me into something. This was exactly what I was looking for, but until that instant I had thought of debating only as a thing to do, not as a place to be. Now I saw a way to connect myself through debating, so I stayed on the team.

The debate office became my second home. I certainly didn't set the debating world on fire, but throughout my college years I had somewhere to go, something to guide me, someplace to connect me. I don't think I could've done as well as I did in college without it. I know that it seems a small thing. But however modest debating is in the bigger picture, it meant the world to me.

So I concur with making our kids feel connected. I experienced it myself. There's no debating it: reach out at home; outreach at school. It is crucial not to let our kids drift away, isolated and aimless. We must keep them in some loop, any loop. That, more than anything else, will give them a fighting chance to grow, to learn, and to succeed.

COMMUNITY—JWS

128

A DEEPER DIALOGUE

Hobbies seem to have given way under the pressure to be in the know. Pastimes have become pursuits to stay abreast of all the latest, edgiest trends and news. It's the necessity we feel to be able to converse, to perform in public, to learn our part, to hold up our end, which turn our hobbies into homework.

I enjoy tramping around old, untended cemeteries—the ones flanking the foundations of tumbledown churches or those hidden behind high grass just off of a backcountry blacktop. There are always interesting recent headstones standing straight, polished, and shiny amid a weathered and worn congregation of older memorials. But I really prefer the old ones. They're more likely to have intricate stonework cut into them. Highly wrought celestial scenes. Facades of houses and public buildings. Cameos of children and angels. Even the occasional statuette of a soldier or a saint. But most of all, these older markers are often the root part of a family story being told there in a small corner of a cemetery. Never a complete story, of course, but one that can be read in rough outline, and, sometimes, one that is still being told. I think of it as a conversation across the generations, and I like to imagine what the forebears would think if they could see how the family dialectic was carried forward over time.

I guess you could say this is my hobby. It certainly engrosses me like a hobby. I do it when I can in my spare time, and it helps me keep life and work in perspective. In these old cemeteries, the gravestones lean and subside, tilting towards obscurity. That reminds me, as I stand there in those quiet grounds, that the chattering conversations with which we amuse ourselves and compete for notice day in and day out are but temporary diversions.

Not that our chitchat is unimportant, for indeed it is vital to our enjoyment and well-being. But periodically it's worth reminding ourselves that what really matters is not the breadth of knowledge we can show off in our conversations but the depth of contact we can have by means of our conversations. This is what I take away from these old cemeteries—that our life stories are about a deeper dialogue that can only be heard in quiet moments of careful listening and mindful reflection. COMMUNITY—JWS

129

HANDS-ON HEALING

Alternative medicine is becoming mainstream, with nationwide surveys showing 42 percent of Americans using some form of it. Perhaps one reason is that alternative care practitioners spend more time interacting with patients—on average, 30 minutes per visit, or four times more than traditional care physicians.

There are many medicines to cure what ails us. This is the golden age of the life sciences. We live longer and better than ever before. Yet we can do even more for ourselves, for there are many forms of healing. The best tonic is a pill to make us well given with a hug to make us smile.

Lambasting science for putting the scientific above the humanistic is silly. That's what makes science work—isolating variables, comparing test to control, eliminating contaminating factors, focusing on measurable outcomes, maintaining an emotional distance from subjects, being skeptical and incredulous, taking nothing at face value. We live longer and better because scientists are no-nonsense practitioners of the scientific method.

But as people, not subjects in an experiment, we want the human connection along with the hard-nosed cure. We need what feels good to us as much as we need what science has proven to be really good for us. So more and more, we're going after it. What truly makes this a golden age is that we needn't ditch one for the other. When science falls short with the human touch, or vice versa, we can stitch the two together. This is what's so extraordinary about the age in which we live—this unprecedented opportunity of ours to weave a whole cloth of well being. Indeed, being well is a responsibility we share with our

doctors. Healing comes from everything we make, not just
from the pills we take.

130

THE GIVE-AWAY

*In a nationwide Yankelovich survey, 74 percent of Americans
agreed that, "Even though there's a lot going on in my life, I wish
there were more occasions for sharing a real sense of elation
and inspiration with others."*

A tradition in many Native American cultures was the
"give-away." When someone had had a major success,
rather than receive the awards and recognition of others,
that person provided gifts to those around him (that could
include everything that one owned). The give-away has
been adapted in modern times by some Native Americans
in the Midwest as the awards ceremony at their basketball
tournaments. Instead of the winning team receiving honors, each team member gives a quilt handmade by someone in his or her family to a person who has inspired them
or helped them succeed. The give-away takes place at the

closing ceremony of the tournament and honors parents, teachers, friends, and relatives. The honorees are presented with the quilts, and they then dance around the gym floor wearing the quilts around their shoulders.

It's not enough to work in isolation. It's not enough to have time to play. It's not even enough to win a competition. Without a sense of community, without fellow workers and players, and without a connection with those who have nurtured us, we are incomplete. COMMUNITY—RKJ

131

A THIRD CHOICE

A national survey conducted by Yankelovich found that 73 percent of Americans would prefer to die at home if given the choice. In point of fact, however, 75 percent of Americans die in a medical facility.

Is cure or care an either/or? Can a good cure never be good care? Both are life affirming—the cure to save life and the care to make life more comfortable. We want both of these things. This is why it makes us sick at heart if it turns out that the cures we've put ourselves through have done little, if anything, to help us—because we wind up with nothing to offset the loss of comfort and care we've had to suffer through. Dying at the hospital when we'd prefer to die at home is a particularly poignant instance of this.

Choosing between care and cure is dauntingly difficult, and a false dichotomy besides. There is a third choice—which is to infuse lots of good care into what we undergo as we take the cure. Maybe then we wouldn't find statistics about dying in the hospital instead of at home so disturbing. The real answer is about balance—making sure the cure comes with lots of care. This is true of everything, including work and life.

There is no either/or to work and life, even though that's the way we often pose the choices available to us. This makes us worry over a false choice between time spent at work versus time spent with life. Work is an integral part of how we live our lives. Indeed, how could we live without it? So our challenge is not work or life. Not life instead of work. Not the trap of that false choice. Rather, our challenge is to infuse as much life as we can into our work, to saturate work with life. This goal is an achievable ambition, indeed, a more reasonable, workable solution we can live with. FULFILLMENT—JWS

132

THE POWER OF IMAGINATION

The progressive abandonment of the imagination begins in childhood.—Elizabeth Sewell

Kid's schedules are often tighter than many adult schedules nowadays. Soccer practice after school on Mondays; ballet on Tuesdays; church youth group on Wednesdays; violin lessons on Thursdays; to say nothing of accelerated math classes. No longer is there time for talking to the baseball as we throw it against the garage door. No longer is there time to produce a backyard drama, or create an imaginary universe. Certainly, there is little time for a child to imagine how they might help make this world a better place.

The movie *Pay It Forward* tells the story of a teacher (played by Kevin Spacey) who challenges his seventh grade class to imagine a project that might change our world and then to put that project into action. The teacher doesn't actually expect much. But one of his students, Trevor McKinney, takes the assignment to heart. He proposes a plan of paying it forward, of doing something for somebody else that they can't do for themselves—and then asking them to pay it forward, to do a generous act for three others. In this way goodness might be multiplied exponentially.

As you might expect, there are complications as Trevor implements his plan, but the power of the boy's imagination ultimately has a ripple effect both in his own family and across the nation. Though set realistically in Las Vegas, the movie is meant as a fable. It invites us to suspend our cynicism, if only for two hours, and experience the compelling power of goodness. And for many moviegoers, it worked. For at a deep level, the message rings true. By taking the time to imagine a better way, Trevor has paid us forward too.   FULFILLMENT—RKJ

133
A QUESTION OF BELIEF

In a nationwide survey commissioned by the New York Times covering a wide range of beliefs and values, no significant differences were found between Catholics and Protestants. On the other hand, differences were found between frequent church attendees and non-attendees. The mere fact of belief appears to matter more than the particulars of belief.

The courage to believe is the hardest thing to muster up. In our modern era of skepticism and irony, what stands out more than the specifics of any particular belief versus another is the ability to have faith in anything at all. It is important, indeed audacious, just to believe. Notwithstanding our contemporary cultural presumption of disbelief, here and there we are able to see and appreciate the impact of belief, even if it's nothing but the belief in oneself. Top sales people know that believing you can sell something no matter the odds is the fundamental prerequisite for breakthrough performance. Medical researchers have documented the healing power of belief. Placebos, prayer, and a positive outlook, they have found, all matter. Star athletes seek the counsel of sports psychologists to improve their game through focus and belief.

Belief is not easy because it takes a leap of faith beyond the scanty evidence at hand. Lately, though, we've begun to find more of the mettle it takes to do this, moving past a simple faith in ourselves to a belief in something beyond ourselves. As a result, when we look around we see religion and spirituality on the rise. A new great awakening is nigh as an entire generation struggles as never before with the big questions of meaning and purpose. What difference will this make to us in a marketplace where the spiral of investments seems to pull everything down to nothing but the hard evidence at hand, to nothing other than a financial bottom line? Is there something more that we want from our capital, and if so, how do we get it?

For example, a small number of money managers run funds that invest only in companies with certain records on environmental or human rights issues. Nonfinancial beliefs matter in the management of these funds as much as, if not more than, getting the highest possible return.

Are there beliefs we ourselves hold for which we are willing to accept a slightly lower return on our investments? Or must our beliefs first be quantified to fit into our spreadsheet models before we can truly accept them? Or is this just an irreconcilable conflict of domains? We will face these sorts of hard questions more and more in the years ahead as our quest for belief grows and deepens. The biggest driver of what we decide will be whether we think belief is even a reasonable way of thinking at all. Any leap beyond the numbers will first require this leap of faith—a gut feeling that there is indeed a better way, a broader purpose, a higher calling, something beyond.   FULFILLMENT—JWS

134
THE TIMES OF MY LIFE

When asked in a nationwide survey, which they would pick if they had a choice, 64 percent of respondents picked more time over more money.

Ah, the times of my life—like the summer after college when I drove to Montana from North Carolina to see my girlfriend (now my wife), who was working and acting at a national park hotel. She'd sent me $100 and her car keys, and I made it there in four days driving almost non-stop. My interstate version of Lewis and Clark. My first exposure to Kansas's open plains, Wyoming's windswept range, and Montana's big sky. I discovered A. R. Ammons's poetry at a bookstand along the way. And my wife and I got engaged.

Or the Christmas Days at my parents' house where my two sisters and I gather our families by mid-afternoon every year to celebrate the holiday together. My mother fills the living room with decorations and gifts and trinkets, and my father presides over the generous dinner meal in the formal dining room. It's a feeling of being at home, as if we could all still live there, indeed, had never left, forever welcome and safe and carefree.

Or the evenings I spent studying in the reading room of the old, stately Wilson Library at the University of North Carolina at Chapel Hill. Books lining every wall. The ceiling arching above, flanked by tall windows that let in the moonlight and the night air. The wooden tables rubbed so smooth from generations of students that you almost felt you could absorb knowledge by osmosis just by sitting there.

Or the first time I hiked to the top of the Thunder River Trail and stepped into the Surprise Valley of the Grand Canyon. Looking back behind me, the cliff walls of the Tapeats Amphitheater were spread out in a breathtaking natural vista of shape and color and shadow, a view that has never left my mind's eye.

Or the long weekend early one fall years ago that my wife and I spent at the beach. We'd scraped together our pennies to cram ourselves into a tiny rental condo, but the weather was perfect three days in a row and we felt like we were teenagers again, falling in love while time crept by so slowly we were sure we'd live forever.

Or the day my wife and I went to the animal shelter to adopt a pet, and a cat chose us instead. A small, four-month-old tabby cat that reached its paw through the cage and grabbed my sweater with its claws, anxious to give us its complete devotion and affection.

The times of my life, which mean more to me than

money—times that no amount of money could ever buy. I'll take more of these times over more money any day.

FULFILLMENT—JWS

135

SUNSETS

Surely there is something in the unruffled calm of nature that overawes our little anxieties and doubts; the sight of the deep-blue sky, and the clustering stars above, seem to impart a quiet to the mind.—Jonathan Edwards

"Why is it that you always take ten pictures of the same sunset when we are on vacation?" my wife, Cathy, asks me rhetorically as we look over our photographs. She knows the answer. I am attempting to capture for future enjoyment that "unruffled calm of nature" that has just put my doubts and anxieties temporarily into perspective.

I have always been a sucker for a sunset. When I was a boy, our family took a several-week vacation at the ocean. After a day of sand castles and bodysurfing, we would shower and then drive to a nearby rocky beach to watch the surfers while the sun slowly set on the water. As I saw the sun complete its circuit, all seemed well. Though there was no speech, the heavens nevertheless were imparting rich knowledge, even to a grade-school boy.   FULFILLMENT—RKJ

136

PREPARED FOR PRAYER

When peace like a river, attendeth my way,
When sorrow like sea billows roll;
Whatever my lot, thou hast taught me to say,
It is well, it is well with my soul.
—Horatio Spafford (opening verse of the hymn,
"It Is Well with My Soul")

Horatio Spafford was a successful lawyer who lost almost everything in the great Chicago fire of 1871 when Mrs. O'Leary's cow kicked over a lantern. He sent his wife and four daughters to Europe to recuperate from the ordeal, but their ship, the Ville du Hauvre, sank in the Atlantic. His daughters drowned; only his wife was rescued. As Spafford sailed to England to meet his wife, he stood on deck watching the waves and wrote this hymn as a prayer to his God.

There will be times for us all when we discover that life does not fit our agendas. It doesn't take a series of tragedies as sobering as those that afflicted Spafford to bring us to our knees. But once we are on our knees, we need to have prepared our souls so that we know to whom we are addressing our cry. A life of prayer best precedes our perceived need for it. FULFILLMENT—RKJ

137
REVERENCE FOR LIFE

I have found the paradox that if I love until it hurts, then there is no hurt, but only more love.—Mother Teresa

Albert Schweitzer won the Nobel Peace Prize in 1952. A musician, medical doctor, theologian, scientist, and humanitarian, Schweitzer lived most of his adult life in Africa, establishing medical facilities there. He believed we each have an obligation to live for more than ourselves, that we should sacrifice a portion of our lives for others.

Schweitzer summed up his philosophy with the phrase "reverence for life."

If you want contemporary examples, think of Jimmy Carter and his support of Habitat for Humanity, Paul Newman and his charitable company that started out by making salad dressing, Dave Winfield and the large number of baseball tickets he donated to city kids to come watch him play, Marva Leno and her efforts on behalf of women in Afghanistan, Eleanor Roosevelt and her commitment to human rights, or Martin Sheen and his faithful protest against nuclear weapons. Life has a necessary dimension beyond ourselves. FULFILLMENT—RKJ

BIBLIOGRAPHY

BALANCE
1 Leonardo da Vinci, as adapted from citation in Charly Heavenrich, *Dancing on the Edge: A Veteran Guide Shares the Transforming Power of the Grand Canyon* (Boulder, Colorado: Beyond the Edge Publishing, 1998), xiv.
2 M. C. Richards, *Centering: In Pottery, Poetry, and the Person* (Middletown, Connecticut: Wesleyan University Press, 1989), 6.
3 Original translation for this book by Gwen Herder of Rainer Maria Rilke, *Sonnets to Orpheus,* First Part, Number 3, February 2-5, 1922, at Chateau de Muzot.
4 George Valliant, *Adaptation to Life* (Boston: Little Brown, 1977), 373.
5 Adapted from Edward Helmore, "Health: The American Dream," *Vogue,* April 2000, 304.
6 Attributed to Stephen Leacock, *The Boy I Left Behind Me* (1947), in *The Oxford Dictionary of Phrase, Saying, & Quotation* (Oxford, England: Oxford University Press, 1997), ed. Elizabeth Knowles, 247.
7 Adapted from William Wordsworth, "Lines Composed a Few Miles Above Tintern Abbey" (1798), in *The Complete Poetical Works of William Wordsworth, Cambridge Edition* (Boston: Houghton Mifflin, 1904), 91.
8 Adapted from Karl Taro Greenfield, "A New Way of Giving," *Time,* 24 July 2000, 48-51; and adapted from Karl Taro Greenfield, "Giving Billions Isn't Easy Bill and Melinda Gates," *Time,* 24 July 2000, 52-55.
9 Augustine, *City of God* (New York: Harner Publishing Co., 1948), 341, tr. Marcus Dodd.
10 Dietrich Bonhoeffer, "Thoughts on the Baptism of D. W. R.," *Letters and Papers from Prison* (New York: Macmillan, 1967), 155.
11 Adapted from T. S. Eliot, "The Dry Salvages," V (27-33), in *Four Quartets* (New York: Harcourt, Brace & Co., 1947), 27.
12 From Robert L. Short, *The Gospel According to Peanuts* (Richmond, Virginia: John Knox Press, 1965), 112.
13 Adapted from Stephen Battaglio, "TV, Napster and the 29.8-Hour Day," at www.inside.com, 27 June 2000.
14 Adapted from Rob Gurwitt, "Slowdown," *DoubleTake,* Summer 1997, 101.
15 Attributed to Bruce Grocott, *Observer,* 22 May 1988, in *The Oxford Dictionary of Phrase, Saying, & Quotation* (Oxford, England: Oxford University Press, 1997), ed. Elizabeth Knowles, 483.

TIME

16 Attributed to Benjamin Franklin, *Advice to a Young Tradesman* (1748), in *The Oxford Dictionary of Phrase, Saying, & Quotation* (Oxford, England: Oxford University Press, 1997), ed. Elizabeth Knowles, 438.

17 Adapted from Pam Belluck, "Parents Try to Reclaim Their Children's Time," *New York Times*, 13 June 2000, A14, national edition.

18 Adapted from John P. Robinson and Geoffrey Godbey, *Time for Life: The Surprising Ways Americans Use Their Time* (University Park, Pennsylvania: The Pennsylvania State University Press, 1997), 27.

19 E. F. Schumacher, *Good Work* (New York: Harper and Row, 1979), 25.

WORK

21 Adapted from Joe Sharkey, "Business Travel," *New York Times*, 10 May 2000, C8.

22 Ghandi, as quoted in Timothy Jack Ward, "Great Words from Great Cheapskates," *New York Times*, 21 September 1995, B6.

23 Richard Livingstone, as quoted in John Templeton, *Worldwide Laws of Life*, (Philadelphia: Templeton Foundation Press, 1997), 469; and adapted from William Morris, ed., *The American Heritage Dictionary of the English Language* (New York: The American Heritage Publishing Company, Inc., and Boston: Houghton Mifflin Company, 1969, 1970), 1435.

24 Adapted from Leslie Wayne, "If It's Tuesday, This Must Be My Family," *New York Times*, 14 May 1995, section 3, 1.

25 Adapted from Robert E. Lane, *The Loss of Happiness in Market Democracies* (New Haven, Connecticut: Yale University Press, 2000), 61.

26 Joseph Sittler, *Gravity and Grace: Reflections & Provocations* (Minneapolis: Augsburg Publishing House, 1986), 35.

27 Adapted from Lisa Girion, "Building the Dream on Overtime," *Los Angeles Times*, 29 October 2000, W1, W4.

28 Adapted from the obituary for David Merrick, *New York Times*, 27 April 2000, A28.

29 Rick Bass, *Winter: Notes from Montana* (New York and Boston: Houghton Mifflin/Seymour Lawrence, 1991), 162.

LIVING

30 *Shall We Dance?* (Director: Suo, 1996.)

31 The TBWA/Chiat Day—Yankelovich Partners New American Dream survey, 1997.

32 From Izaak Walton, as quoted in Roy Rowan, "Solitude: The Power of One," *Bottom Line Personal,* 1 April 2000, 9.

33 Adapted from Karen Peterson, "Neighborly Neighbors Are the Norm, Poll Shows," *USA Today,* 14 July 1997, D1.

34 Adapted from Stephanie Armour, "Breakfast Eats Time, So Workers Gobble at the Office," *USA Today,* 22 June 2000, B6.

35 Adapted from Philip Shenon, "Top Guns Quitting for Life at Cruising Altitude," *New York Times,* 22 October 1997, A10, national edition.

36 Adapted from Alan Wolfe, "The Pursuit of Autonomy," *New York Times Magazine,* 7 May 2000, 56.

38 The description of the Princeton experiment is adapted from Peter Steinfels, "Beliefs," *New York Times,* 13 March 2000, A12, national edition.

39 Peter Gomes, *The Good Book: Reading the Bible with Mind and Heart* (New York: William Morrow, 1996), 201.

40 Adapted from Maria Puente, "Students Get Lesson in 'Road Rage'," *USA Today,* 16 October 1997, A3; and adapted from Alan Levin, "'Air Rage' A Threat on Flights," *USA Today,* 12 June 2000, A1.

41 James D. Walsh, M.D., as quoted in John Templeton, *Worldwide Laws of Life* (Philadelphia: Templeton Foundation Press, 1997), 159.

42 Adapted from Andrea Atkins, "Laughing Matters," *World Traveler,* November 1996, 53; and adapted from Elizabeth Ellis, in *The Storyteller's Guide* (Little Rock, Arkansas: August House, Inc., 1996), 68-69.

43 Kurt Vonnegut, *Mother Night* (New York: Dell Publishing, 1961, 1966), v.

PLAY

45 Adapted from Teresa Riordan, "Patents," *New York Times,* 22 May 2000, C8, national edition; and adapted from Edward Iwata, "Tech's Tyranny Provokes Revolt," *USA Today,* 21 August 2000, A1.

46 Attributed to Eric Gill, *Art-nonsense and Other Essays* (1929), in *The Oxford Dictionary of Phrase, Saying, & Quotation* (Oxford, England: Oxford University Press, 1997), ed. Elizabeth Knowles, 482-483.

47 Walter Kerr, *The Decline of Pleasure* (New York: Simon & Shuster, 1962), 39-40, 48.

48 Adapted from Ellen Graham and Cynthia Crossen, "The Overloaded American: Too Many Things to Do, Too Little Time to Do Them," *Wall Street Journal,* 8 March 1996, R1.

49 Adapted from Debra Galant, "Now for the Hard Part: It's Over," *New York Times,* 12 July 2000, H12, final city edition.

50 John Huizinga, *Homo Ludens: A Study of the Play Element in Culture,* (Boston: Beacon Press, 1955), 7.

51 Edward M. Hallowell, M.D., *Connect: Vital Ties That Open Your Heart, Lengthen Your Life, and Deepen Your Soul* (New York: Pantheon Books, 1999), 21.

SPIRITUALITY

52 The Yankelovich Monitor®, 1976 and the Yankelovich Monitor OmniPlus, 1998.

53 George Gallup, Jr. and Timothy Jones, *The Next American Spirituality: Finding God in the Twenty-First Century* (Colorado Springs, Colorado: Cook Communications, Victor Books, 2000), 184.

54 Adapted from Richard Eder, "Books of the Times," *New York Times,* 24 August 2000, B7, national edition.

55 Adapted from Rita Carter, *Mapping the Mind* (Berkeley, California: University of California Press, 1998), 11.

56 Adapted from Richard Willing, "Under Law, Pets Are Becoming Almost Human," *USA Today,* 13 September 2000, A2.

57 George Bernanos, *The Diary of a Country Priest* (New York: The MacMillan Co., 1937), 25, tr. P. Morris.

WHOLENESS

58 The Yankelovich Monitor CnXn survey, 1996.

59 Henry Grunwald, *Twilight: Losing Sight, Gaining Insight* (New York: Alfred A. Knopf: 1999), 128.

60 Man Ray, as quoted in curator's commentary for an exhibition of his photography at the Walker Art Center, Minneapolis, Minnesota, June 2000; and William McDonough, as quoted in Roger Rosenblatt, "A Whole New World: The Man Who Wants Buildings to Love Kids," *Time,* 22 February 1999, 70-73.

61 Adapted from William Morris, ed., *The American Heritage Dictionary of the English Language* (New York: The American Heritage Publishing Co., Inc., and Boston: Houghton Mifflin Company, 1969, 1970), 194.

62 Adapted from Kathleen Dean Moore, *Riverwalking: Reflections on Moving Water* (New York: Harcourt Brace, 1995), 14.

63 Henry David Thoreau, *Walden and Other Writings of Henry David Thoreau* (New York: The Modern Library, 1937), ed. Brooks Atkinson, 101.

EMPOWERMENT

64 Adapted from Maria Puente, "Multi-tasking to the Max: The Only Thing You Can't Do at the Same Time is Smell the Roses," *USA Today,* 25 April 2000, D1.

65 Adapted from Ellen Graham and Cynthia Crossen, "The Overloaded American: Too Many Things to Do, Too Little Time to Do Them," *Wall Street Journal,* 8 March 1996, R4.

67 Adapted from Dylan Loeb McClain, "Forget the Raise, Give Me Some Time Off," *New York Times,* 12 July 2000, G1, final city edition.

68 The Yankelovich Monitor, 2000.

69 Adapted from bar chart, "Life Expectancy Through Time," *USA Today,* 17 March 1999, D5.

70 Hamilton Jordan in *No Such Thing as a Bad Day* (Atlanta: Longstreet Press, 2000), as quoted in Margaret Carlson, "Rudy, This Book's for You," *Time,* 22 May 2000, 37.

71 Stanley Hauerwas, "The Sanctified Body: Why Perfection Does Not Require a Soul," in *Embodied Holiness: Toward a Corporate Theology of Spiritual Growth* (Downers Grove, Illinois: InterVarsity Press, 1999) eds. Samuel M. Powell and Michael E. Lodahl, 33.

72 Joey Reiman, *The Best Year of Your Life: Make It Happen Now!* (Atlanta: Longstreet Press, 1996), 52.

JOY

75 Craig Childs, *Crossing Paths: Uncommon Encounters with Animals in the Wild* (Sasquatch Books: Seattle, Washington, 1997), 91-92.

76 Stephanie Crouse, as quoted in Stephanie Armour, "Breakfast Eats Time, So Workers Gobble at the Office," *USA Today,* 22 June 2000, B6.

77 Webster's II New Riverside Dictionary (New York: Berkley Publishing Group, 1984), 535.

STRESS

78 Adapted from Steven Holmes, "Children Study Longer and Play Less, a Report Says," *New York Times,* 11 November 1998, National section; and adapted from Jacques Barzun, *From Dawn to Decadence: 1500 to the Present* (New York: HarperCollins, 2000), 84.

79 For example, see links and resources on medical conditions and stress at: http://stress.about.com/health/stress/cs/medical conditions/.

80 Adapted from Sandra Blakeslee, "Placebos Prove So Powerful Even Experts Are Surprised," *New York Times,* 13 October 1998, D4.

MATERIALISM

81 Adapted from Gayle White, "Consumed by Consumerism," *Atlanta Journal-Constitution,* 13 December 1998, R1.

82 "Snapshot: If I Were a Rich Man," *USA Today,* 24 October 1997, A1.

83 Adapted from Andrew Goldstein, "Paging All Parents," *Time,* 3 July 2000, 47.

84 Adapted from Deal Hudson, "A Religious Revival," *Wall Street Journal,* 20 March 1998, W13.

85 Charles Dickens, *A Tale of Two Cities* (Westport, CT: the Easton Press, 1975), 1; and adapted from David G. Myers, *The American Paradox: Spiritual Hunger in an Age of Plenty* (New Haven, CT: Yale University Press, 2000), 1–3.

86 Adapted from Jeffrey Nesteruk, "My Money, My Life: Don't Be Shocked, But Money Isn't Everything," *New York Times,* 10 January 1999, Money and Business section, 4.

87 Adapted from Ellen Graham and Cynthia Crossen, "The Overloaded American: Too Many Things to Do, Too Little Time to Do Them," *Wall Street Journal,* 8 March 1996, R1.

88 Adapted from Elliott Abrams, "A Religious Revival," *Wall Street Journal,* 20 March 1998, W13.

89 Adapted from Joe Stevens, "Are You A Loser?" *Pasadena Star News,* 25 July 2000, D1.

90 Adapted from Carey Goldberg, "The Simple Life Lures Refugees From Stress," *New York Times,* 21 September 1995, B6.

91 Adapted from Kirsten Gerencher, "Keep Your Lifeline Regis," CBSMarketWatch.com, 16 May 2000; and adapted from Evelyn Nieves, "Many in Silicon Valley Cannot Afford Housing, Even at $50,000 a Year," *New York Times,* 20 February 2000, National Section.

REPOSE

92 Nathaniel Hawthorne, as quoted in John Templeton, *Worldwide Laws of Life* (Philadelphia: Templeton Foundation Press, 1997), 427; and Andrew Delbanco, "Are You Happy Yet?" *New York Times Magazine,* 7 May 2000, 44.

93 Adapted from Michelle Conlin, "Religion in the Workplace," *Business Week,* 1 November 1999, 152.

94 Adapted from Cynthia Crossen, "Solitude Is a Casualty of the War with Time," *Wall Street Journal,* 8 March 1996, R4.

95 Adapted from Epworth Sleepiness Scale as shown at: www.stanford.edu/~dement/Epworth.html.

96 Adapted from Stephanie Armour, "Latest Victim of Downsizing: The Lunch Hour," *USA Today,* 21 November 1997, A1.

WONDER

97 Pearl Buck, as quoted in Rachel Dolin, *A Crown of Glory: A Biblical View of Aging* (New York: Paulist Press, 1988), 3.

98 Michelangelo, as adapted from *The Complete Poetry of Michelangelo,* (Athens, Ohio: Ohio University Press, 1991), ed. and tr. Sidney Alexander, 110.

99 Adapted from David Brower, "Foreword," in Francois Leydet, *Time and the River Flowing* (San Francisco: Sierra Club, 1964), 5.

NURTURE

100 Adapted from Gayle White, "Consumed by Consumerism," *Atlanta Journal-Constitution,* 13 December 1998, R3.

101 Adapted from "Pets and Your Health: The Power of Puppy Love," *Mayo Clinic Health Oasis,* www.mayohealth.org, 20 July 2000.

102 Adapted from Elizabeth Lee, "We're Outta Here," *Atlanta Journal-Constitution,* 2 September 1998, F3.

103 Adapted from Neal Gabler, *Life: The Movie: How Entertainment Conquered Reality* (New York: Alfred A. Knopf, 1998).

104 Adapted from Diane Lore, "Asleep at the Wheel," *Atlanta Journal-Constitution,* 29 March 1998, D6.

HAPPINESS

105 Andrew Delbanco, "Are You Happy Yet?" *New York Times Magazine,* 7 May 2000, 48.

106 Adapted from Michael Gross, "The Lethal Politics of Beauty: Why Women Are Dying to Look This Good," *George,* June 2000, 56.

107 Adapted from Keri Russell, "Keri Russell [of WB show, "Felicity"] Says Fame is Fleeting," www.detnews.com, 28 April 1999.

108 Adapted from Bill Hendrick, "Born to Be Happy?" *Atlanta Journal-Constitution,* 19 October 1996, R1.

109 Eugene N. Peterson, *The Message: The New Testament in Contemporary English* (Colorado Springs, CO: NavPress Publishing Group, 1993), 444.

110 Adapted from Nikhil Deogun, "Top PepsiCo Executive Picks Family Over Job," *Wall Street Journal,* 24 September 1997, B1.

AUTHENTICITY

111 Adapted from Lisa Belkin, "That's Why It's Called Labor Day," *New York Times,* 30 August 2000, G1.

112 Alan Wolfe, "The Pursuit of Autonomy," *New York Times Magazine,* 7 May 2000, 56.

113 The Yankelovich Monitor, 1979 and 1998.

114 President Dwight D. Eisenhower, Renomination Acceptance Speech, 23 August 1956, Republican National Convention, San Francisco; and adapted from Matthew 7:24–27 (NRSV).

115 Adapted from Families and Work Institute, "Executive Summary," *The 1998 Business Work-Life Study: A Sourcebook,* xii, www.familiesandwork.org.

116 Studs Terkel, *Working* (New York: Pantheon Books, 1974), xxiv.

INTEGRITY

117 Adapted from Larry Young, "The Boss: My Mistakes Make ESPN," *New York Times,* 25 October 2000, C8.

119 Adapted from Eileen Daspin, "The Cheater Principle," *Wall Street Journal,* 25 August 2000, W1.

120 Adapted from Andrea Atkins, "Laughing Matters," *World Traveler,* November 1996, 53; and adapted from Jennifer Steinhauer, "Testing a Wider Concept of Sexual Harassment," *New York Times,* 27 March 1997, Business/Financial Section.

COMMUNITY

121 Adapted from Edward M. Hallowell, M.D., *Connect: Vital Ties That Open Your Heart, Lengthen Your Life, and Deepen Your Soul* (New York: Pantheon Books, 1999), 20.

123 Adapted from Gregg Zoroya, "Dinner Traditions Nourish Families," *USA Today,* 15 October 1997, D1.

124 Adapted from Edward M. Hallowell, M.D., *Connect: Vital Ties That Open Your Heart, Lengthen Your Life, and Deepen Your Soul* (New York: Pantheon Books, 1999), 5-6.

125 The Yankelovich Monitor, 1999.

126 Adapted from Nancy Ann Jeffrey, "Whatever Happened to Friendship," *Wall Street Journal,* 3 March 2000, W1; and the Yankelovich Monitor, 2000.

127 Adapted from Edward M. Hallowell, M.D., *Connect: Vital Ties That Open Your Heart, Lengthen Your Life, and Deepen Your Soul* (New York: Pantheon Books, 1999), 7-8.

128 Adapted from Randy Cohen, "Elegy for the Hobby," *New York Times Magazine,* 25 May 1997, 46-47.

129 Adapted from Jane Brody, "Alternative Medicine Makes Inroads, but Watch Out for Curves," *New York Times,* 28 April 1998, F7.

130 The Yankelovich Monitor, 1998.

FULFILLMENT

131 Adapted from Staff and Wire Reports, "Death Wishes Rarely Fulfilled," *USA Today,* 13 September 2000, D6.

132 Elizabeth Sewell, "The Death of the Imagination," *Logos I,* Spring 1997, 180, reprinted from *Thought,* no. 27, 1953, 413-445.

133 Adapted from Alan Wolfe, "The Pursuit of Autonomy," *New York Times Magazine*, 7 May 2000, 56.

134 Adapted from Dylan Loeb McClain, "Forget the Raise, Give Me Some Time Off," *New York Times,* 12 July 2000, G1, final city edition.

135 Jonathan Edwards, as quoted in John Templeton, *Worldwide Laws of Life* (Philadelphia: Templeton Foundation Press, 1997), 427.

136 Horatio Spafford, "It Is Well With My Soul" (1873), *The Covenant Hymnal* (Chicago: Covenant Publications, 1996), 451.

137 Mother Teresa, as quoted in John Templeton, *Worldwide Laws of Life* (Philadelphia: Templeton Foundation Press, 1997), 485; and Albert Schweitzer, *Reverence for Life* (New York: Harper & Row, 1969).

ACKNOWLEDGMENTS

It was Ken and Helen Shaw who asked me to lecture on "The Christian at Play" to a group of psychologists in the San Francisco Bay area. Our editor, Roy M. Carlisle, was in the audience that night. Thus, when his publisher, Tamara Traeder, suggested the title for this book and began brainstorming with Roy concerning its shape and potential author, he thought of my interest and asked if I would consider the project. And so a book was born. I am thus indebted, not only to Tamara and Roy and their team at Wildcat Canyon Press, but to the Shaws.

My first (and perhaps best) decision was to ask Walker Smith to join the project. Over several years at Renaissance Weekends where people across the professions come together with their families to share our lives together and learn from each other, Walker and his wife Joy have become friends with my wife Cathy and myself. His common values and beliefs, together with his encyclopedic knowledge of trends in contemporary life, have made him a much valued colleague on this project. Two friends with quite different geographies (Atlanta and Los Angeles), professions (market research and theological education), and interests (Walker's music library and poetry collection; my love of movies and sports) have written first for each other's benefit. If it has rung true to us, we believe it might hold true for you as well. Thus the book is a true collaboration for which I thank Walker.

Finally, I have not only shared the observations in this book with my wife, Catherine Barsotti, we have lived through many of them. My daughters, Liz and Margi, have also served as an informal panel of judges as to whether a given page worked or not. They are not to be blamed for what is finally included, but you can thank them for what has been eliminated.

—*Robert K Johnston*

I am most indebted by far to my co-author, Rob Johnston. His generosity with the pen provided me with a role in this project, and the example of his writing and thinking has been inspiring, as indeed it always is. I never expected I'd co-author a book like this. It's not my usual style to share private reflections or to confess remorse for having made a public scene, no matter how long ago it took place. More often than not I keep my regrets and my counsel to myself. But when Rob called me unexpectedly one warm spring night and invited me to help with this book, I surprised myself with how quickly I said yes. Perhaps I was just done in by the air of rebirth wafting through my window that night, for working on this book has been a renewal of sorts for me. By writing about my struggle to balance my work with my life, I have been able to finally put to rest a very demanding period in my life. In sharing with me the opportunity to work on this book, Rob has given me a gift for which I am grateful beyond words. Thanks, too, to Cathy Barsotti, his wife, whose excitement about my early drafts was timely encouragement that was very much appreciated.

I owe more thanks than I can say to Roy M. Carlisle whose confidence in me was infectious and whose advice, guidance, support, assistance, coaching, and charity of spirit kept me focused and motivated. Of course, there would have been no book at all without the original idea of Tamara Traeder, who generously welcomed me to this project with open arms and a faith beyond any evidence I had to offer that I had something to contribute. The tireless work of Carol Brown and her colleague Patsy Barich has given this book an opportunity in the marketplace well beyond my wildest fantasies. The careful reading and editing of Jean Blomquist rescued my writing from my usual surfeit of ambiguities and poor grammar. Thanks to everyone at Wildcat Canyon for their support and help along the way, most especially Leyza Yardley for keeping things on track and Larissa Berry for patiently deciphering my illegible edits, and Mary Beth Salmon for designing a spectacular-looking book cover.

My family has supported me without question or reservation through thick and thin. Thanks to my wife Joy, our terrific tabby cat Fred, my parents Jack and Sis, and my sisters Marjorie and Dorothy.

In spite of my periodic moodiness and grousing, my colleagues at Yankelovich have been unfailingly supportive and accepting, especially Marc, Karen, Margaret, and Christine who worked and lived with me through some very long hours during some very intense years. Permission to work on this project was graciously given by Bruce, David, and John, my friends and business associates at WAND Partners. Thanks as well to my good friends, Steve and Max, each of whom has taught me many important things about keeping life in balance.

I am truly blessed by the opportunities in work and life given to me by God, for which I am grateful and thankful above all else. —*J. Walker Smith*

ABOUT THE AUTHORS

Robert K. Johnston, Ph.D. is currently Professor of Theology and Culture at Fuller Theological Seminary in Pasadena, California. He is an ordained minister in the Evangelical Covenant Church. Rob is the author or co-author of nine books, including *The Variety of American Evangelicalism* (1997) and *Reel Spirituality* (2000), as well as more than eighty articles and chapters on topics such as theology and literature, theology and film and the Old Testament. He has taught at Stanford University, Western Kentucky University, Duke University, St. Mark's Seminary, and Fuller Theological Seminary where he has been Provost and Vice-President. He was also Provost of North Park College and Seminary. Dr. Johnston is a Phi Beta Kappa graduate of Stanford University and did his Ph.D. at Duke University on Theology and Play. Rob's wife Cathy is a teacher at a Latino training center for Christian leaders and a consultant to non-profit organizations. Rob and Cathy live in Pasadena, CA.

❀

J. Walker Smith, Ph.D., is president of Yankelovich Partners, Inc., a branding and marketing consultancy specializing in lifestyle trends and customer targeting solutions. Walker is co-author of *Rocking the Ages: The Yankelovich Report on Generational Marketing* (1997), a highly regarded assessment of generational marketing strategies, and a much sought after speaker and authority on social trends in America. Prior to Yankelovich, Walker was director of research for DowBrands, Inc. He is a lecturer at the annual School of Marketing Research at the University of Notre Dame and he is a past vice president of the marketing research division of the American Marketing Association. He serves on numerous corporate and academic boards. Walker earned three degrees from the University of North Carolina at Chapel Hill including a doctorate in Mass Communication Research. Walker's wife Joy is the Atlanta showroom manager for Harvé Benard clothing and an active volunteer for local church and community groups. Walker and Joy live in Atlanta, GA.

ABOUT THE PRESS

Wildcat Canyon Press publishes books that embrace such subjects as friendship, spirituality, women's issues, and home and family, all with a focus on self-help and personal growth. Great care is taken to create books that inspire reflection and improve the quality of our lives. Our books invite sharing and are frequently given as gifts.

For a catalog of our publications, please write:

Wildcat Canyon Press
2716 Ninth Street
Berkeley, California 94710
Phone: (510) 848-3600
Fax: (510) 848-1326
or visit our website at www.wildcatcanyon.com